EPOS

A Song for Alaric

Carlyle Reedy

etruscan books

2013

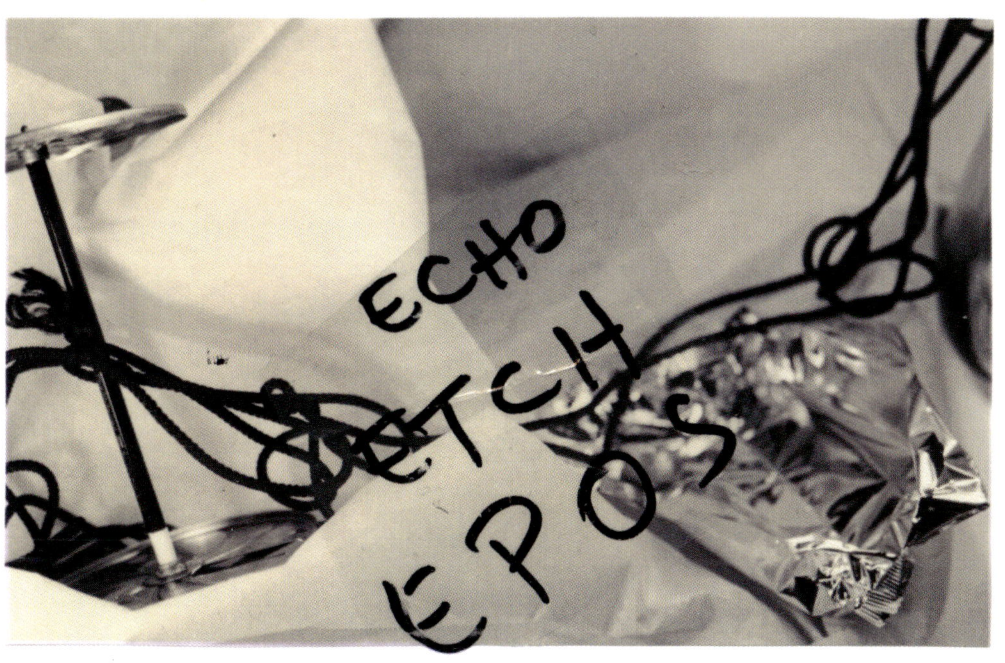

ECHO
ETCH
EPOS

ERNATAL

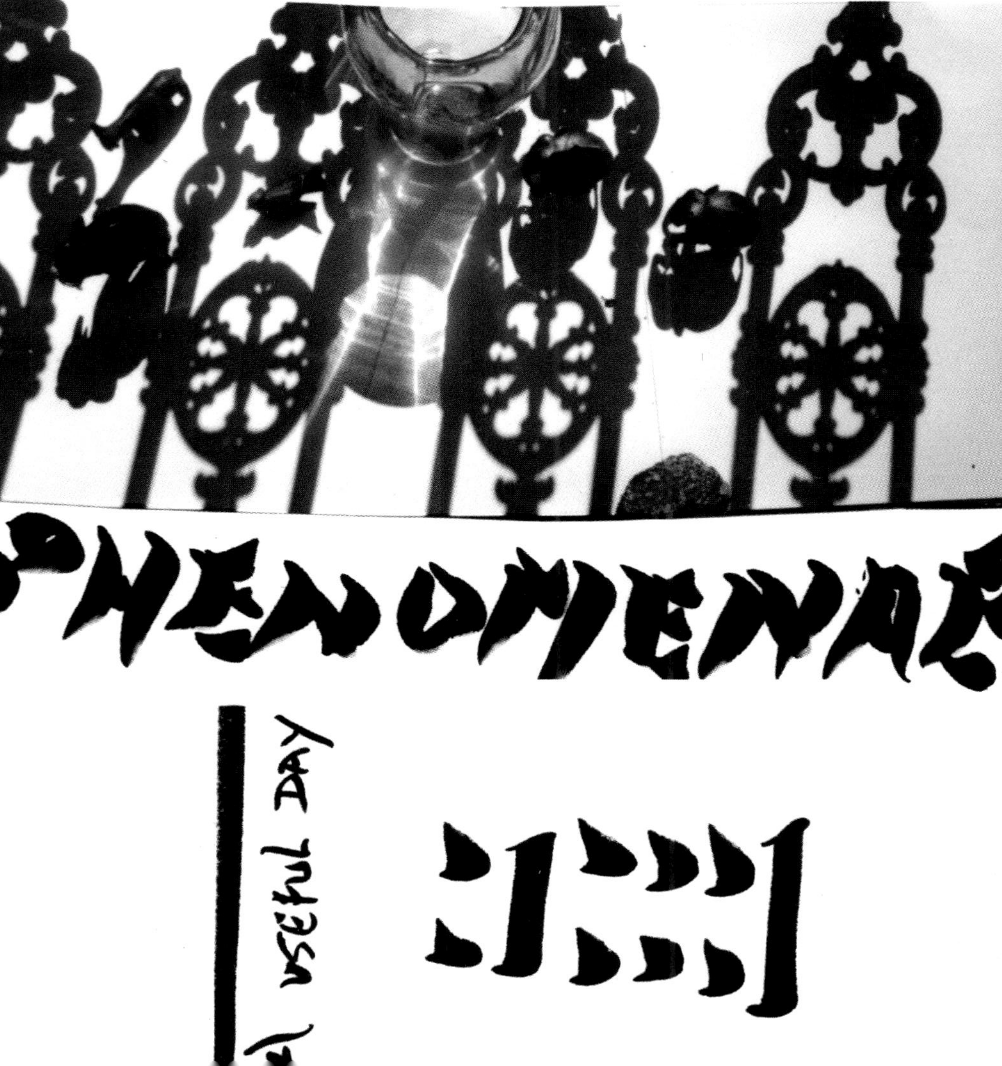

PHENOMENAE

a) USEFUL DAY

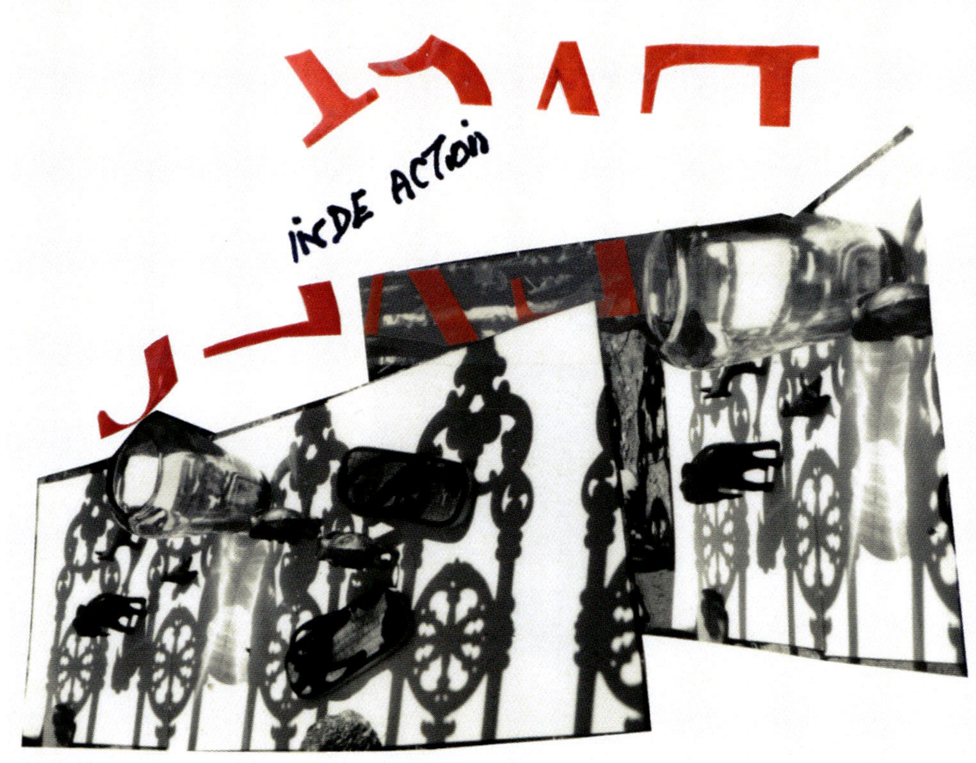

INDE ACTION

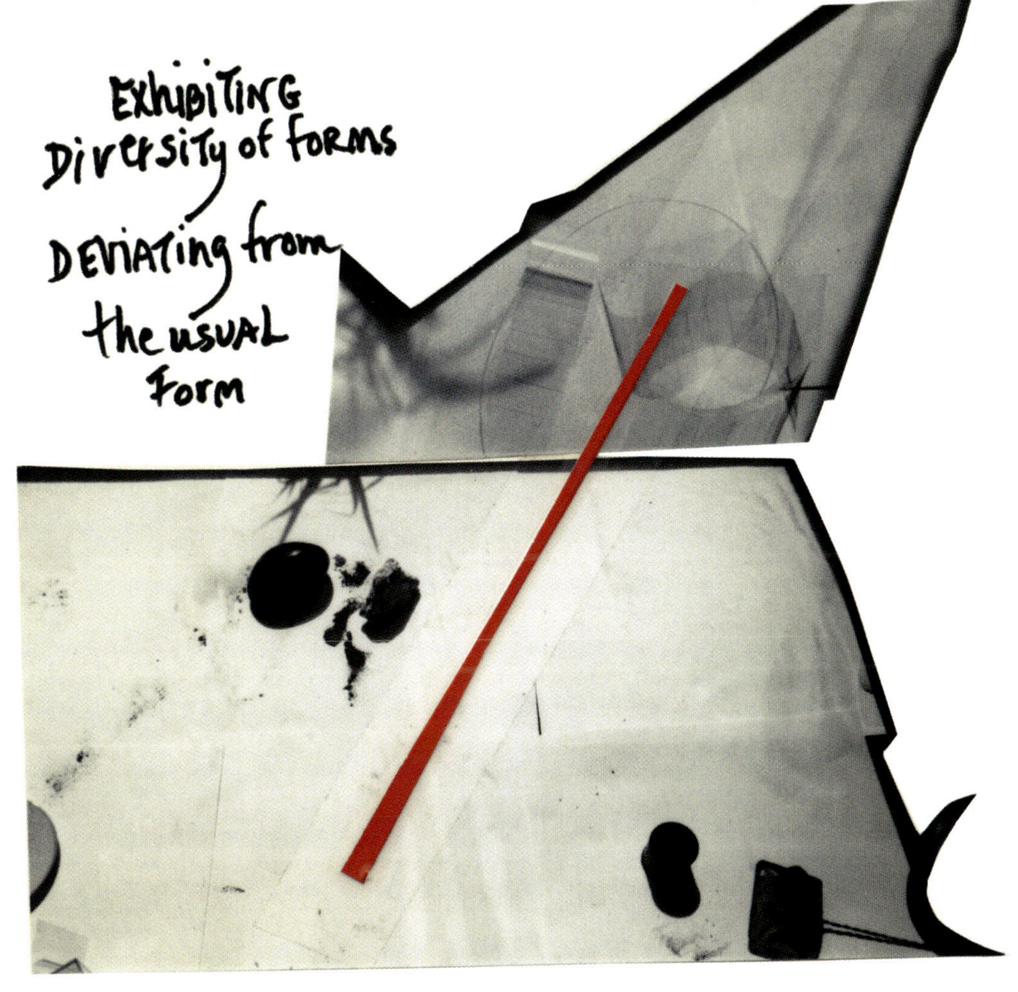
EXHIBITING
DiVERSiTY of FORMS

DEViATiNG from

the USUAL
Form

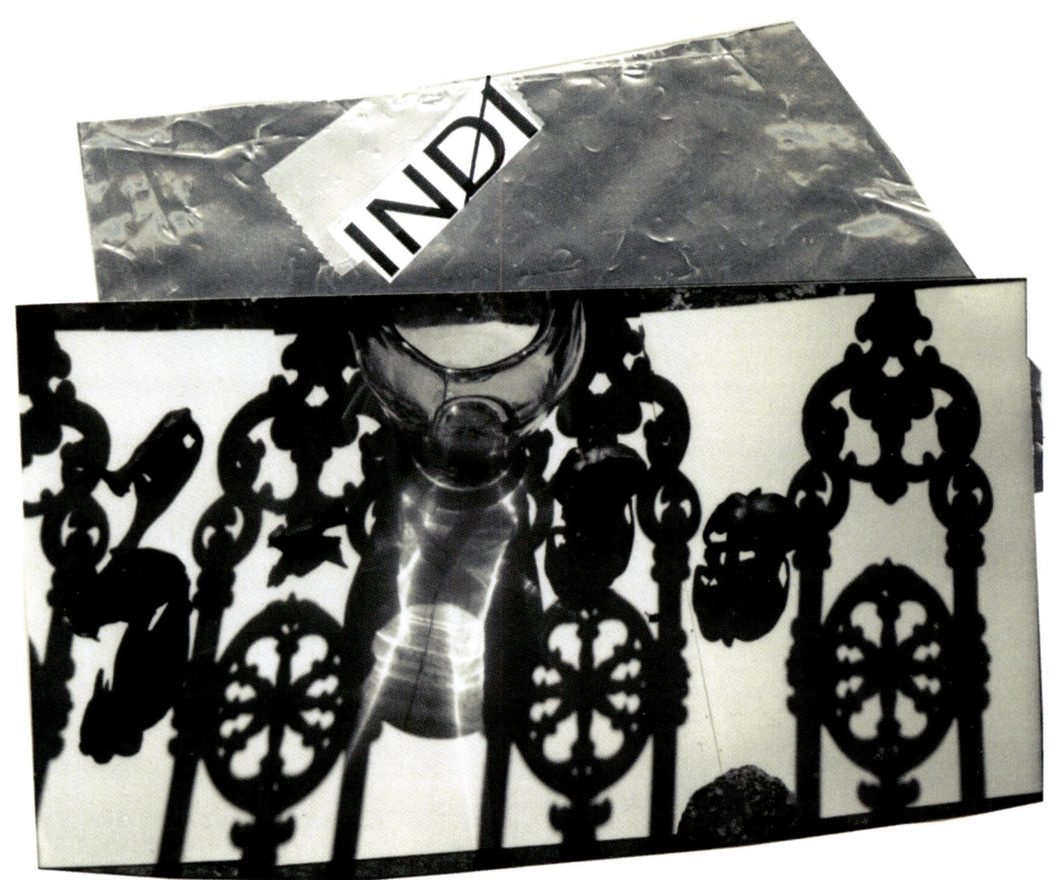
INDI

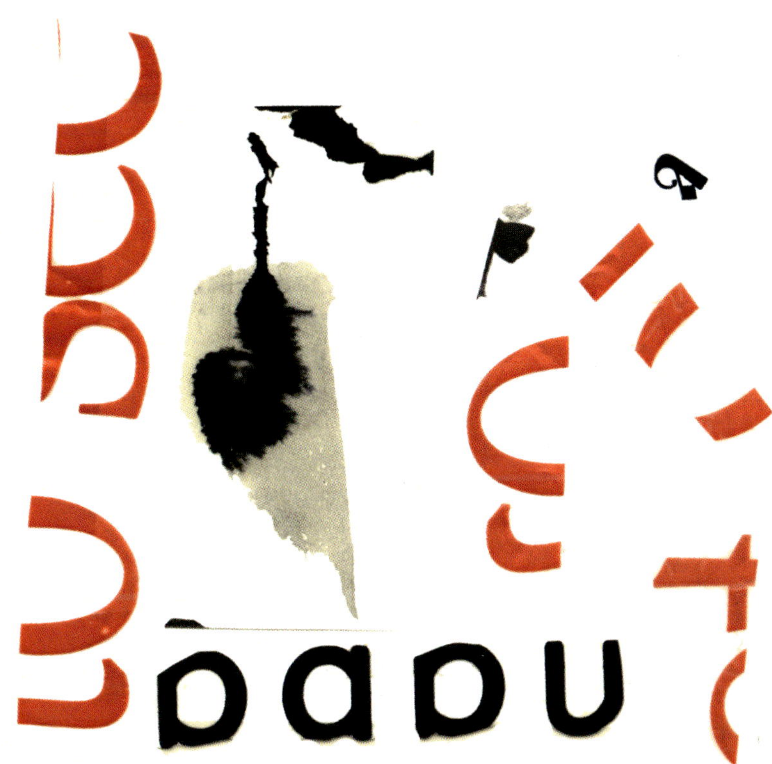

poet tries to squeeze the last sweet juices out of pointless imagery, v
in nothing, philosophy that died with the first A-bomb.

acelsus asked "Why is it that blindness and shortsightedness prevail,"
ented that humans who do not even know the constellation of the whale, t
r of the sea, are too shortsighted to accomplish life. He put it that t
indness and shortsightedness is the Death of the Soul.
s lament
makes a point that knowledge from knowing thru reason/fact/
ach all & everything   that this being so there is no knowledge where t
no social accountability, no respect, which like faith is not purchasea

y do I make the correlation between knowledge which does not reach all a
ing and social accountability. Marx did the same t

ds become   hyperbole, art appreciated for mean   sons", du
re fat tomes of dead philosophical discourse are   The resou
epathy, silence, being now

ing   now, the poet   peaks thr
erial world has to use old toys   is driven to s   omfull of
the idea of communication lurking there
poet deliberately unnerves   other people in the room by saying nothi
y getting so pissed as to be incapable of doing anything "right" or be
ocatory "mad" speech.
              reach a goal by doing   what appears at first to
ely away from it.

value for the poets in adversity with language   impoverished, allied
lead histories, systems of oppression and money, is that these are thro
themselves to discover inner resilience and resources always greater t
irst imagined.
mpting to work in terms of   language, the poets handle it, call it t
twist it and turn it, but often all the same it stares back at them wit
. Even the obscurantist constructions and all the flipping and destruc
guage become a game...

EEE

POSITION

U

é

NT USE LANGUAGE

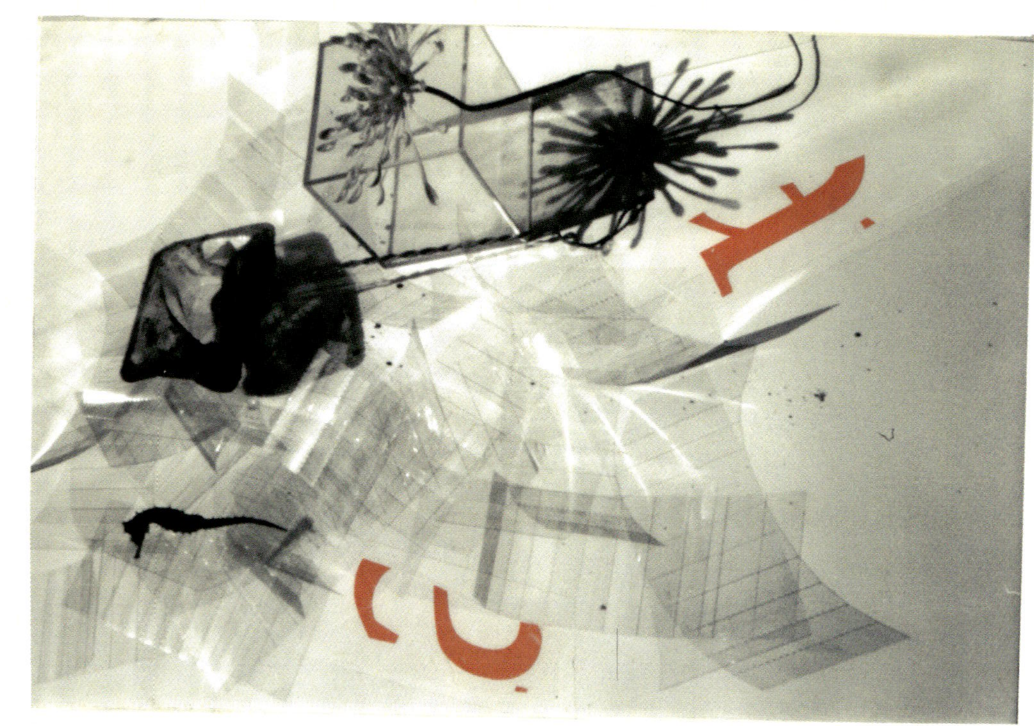

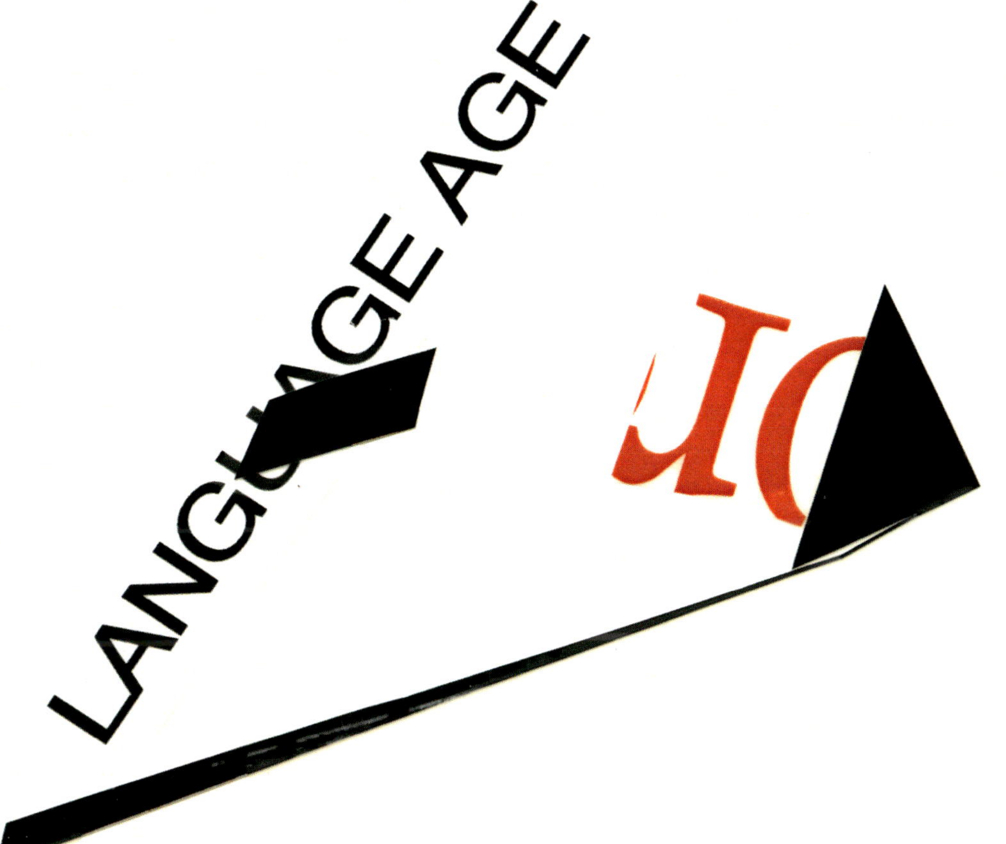

LANGUAGE AGE
AGE

electrons   slow   collide with nitrogen (?) gas
kinetic (fast) so the electron is knocked off

(this)(?) equals = an ION

if IONS   annode   cathode (then)
I can't read it   Neg

Xenon
                              Energy
Argon
                              Jewels

HELIUM   c opy by hand

EMISSION   Sodium cloride
                    (SALT) heated in a bunson
                                        EMITS Light
NEON   yellow sodium   Street Lamps
    spectre scope shows   Separate lines of different
                           (a line emission spectrum?)
sodium calcium berium, each has a characteristic set
Line emission spectra can be studied to discover
whether it is sodium calcium berium whatever

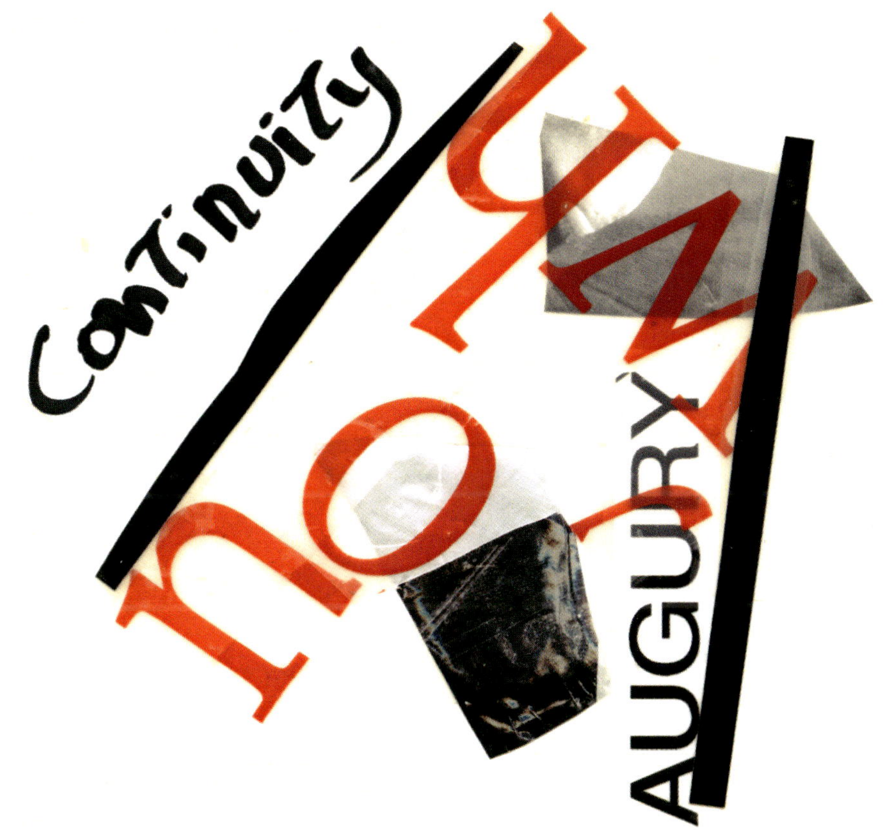
Continuity
URN
AUGURY

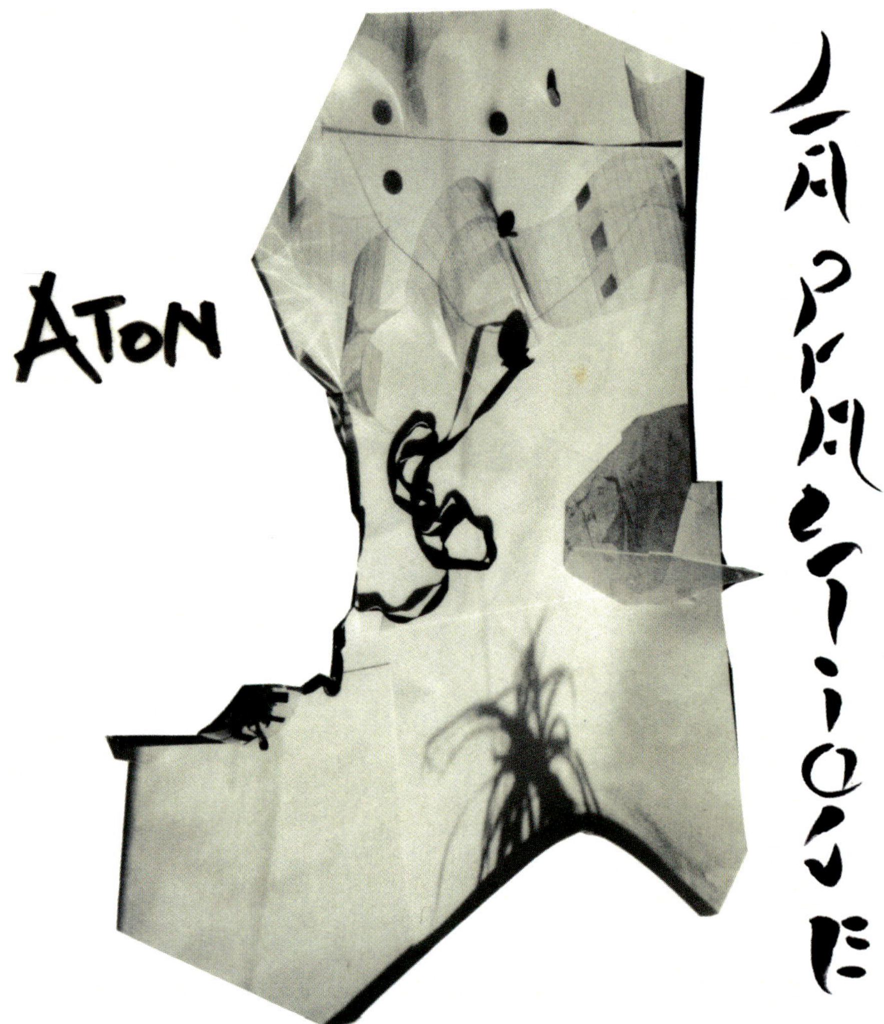

ATON

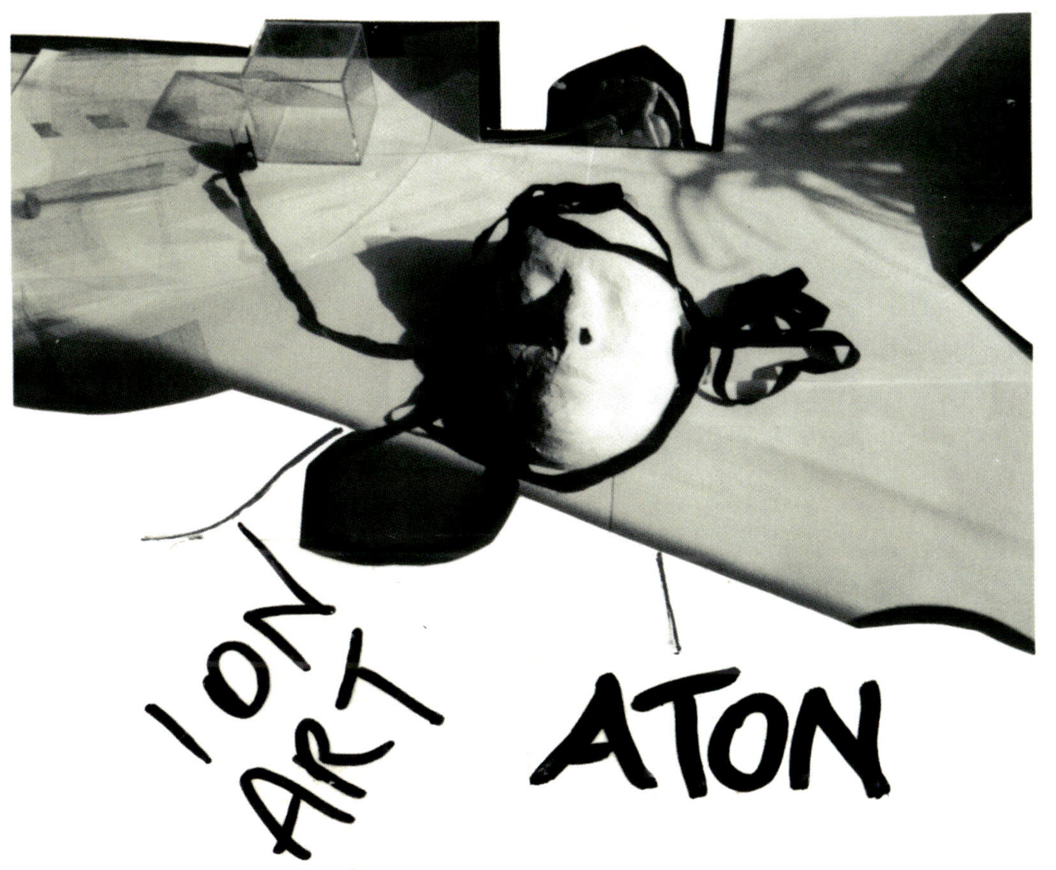
ION
ART
ATON

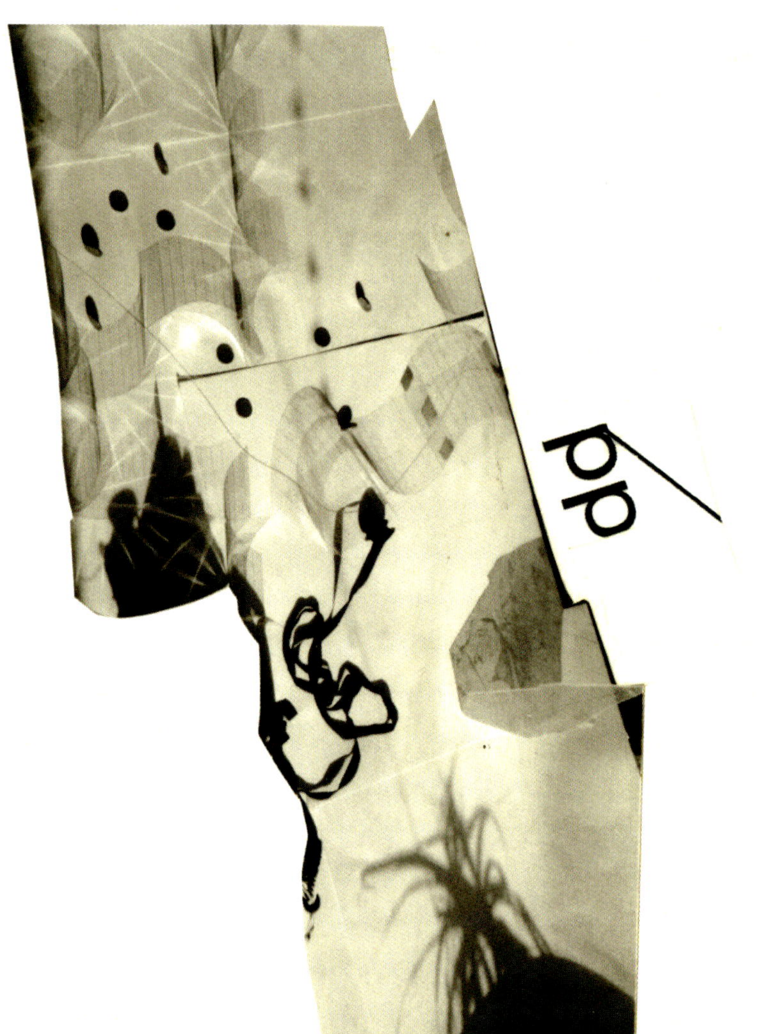

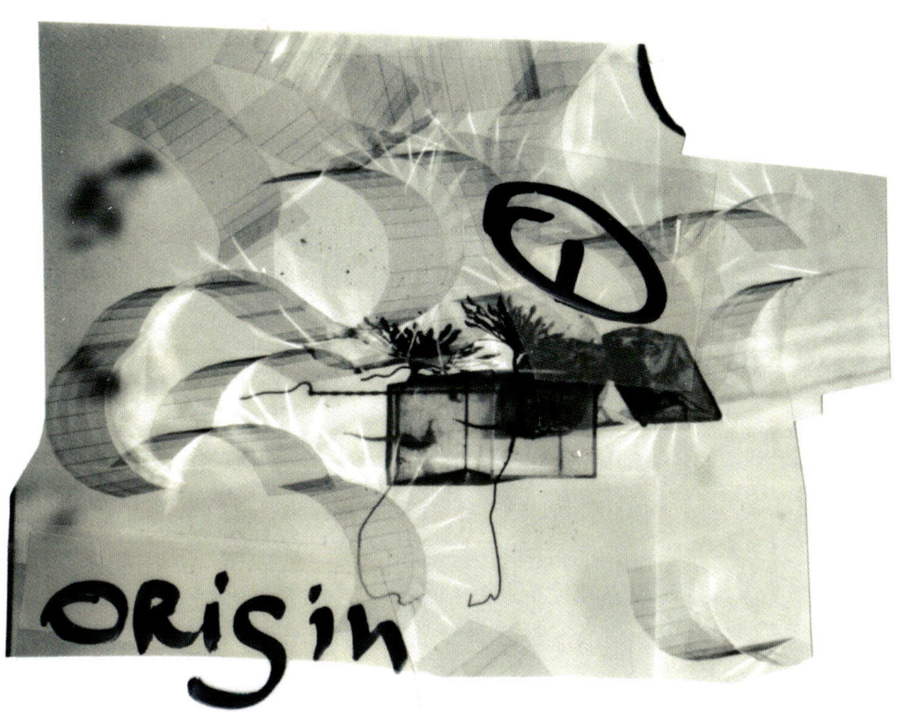
ORIgin

Crab Rag Rich

Roll Rive Crack

Plage Nowl Hire

Lips Slip Lisp Rich

Vague Wabe

Repet scoil Res

Vrack

Luck

Flame

Roove

Brim

lende

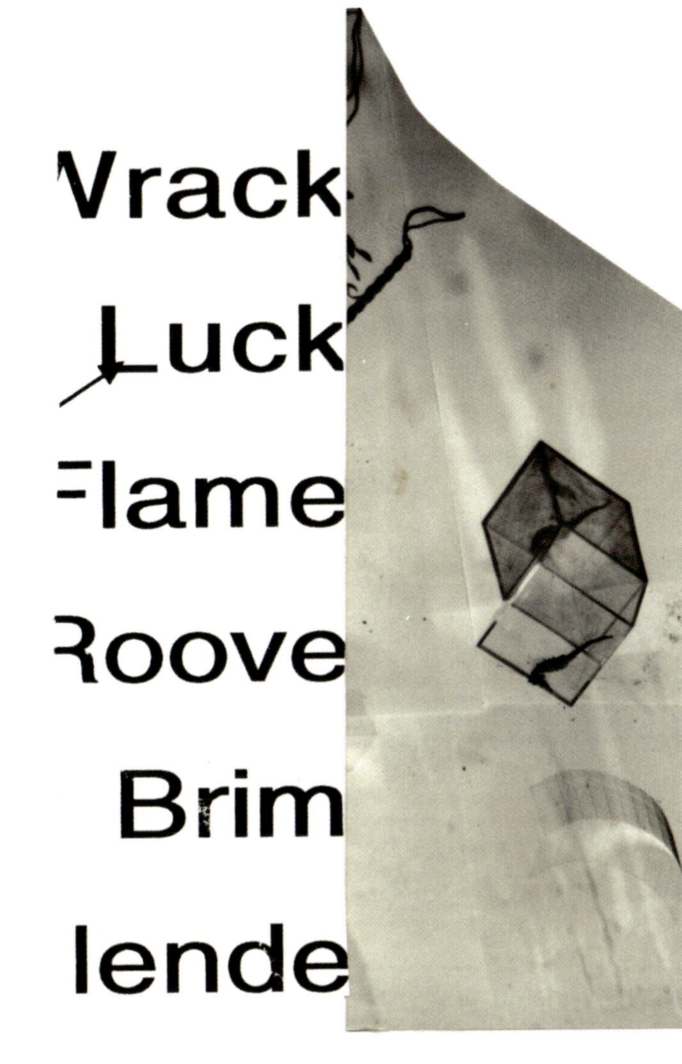

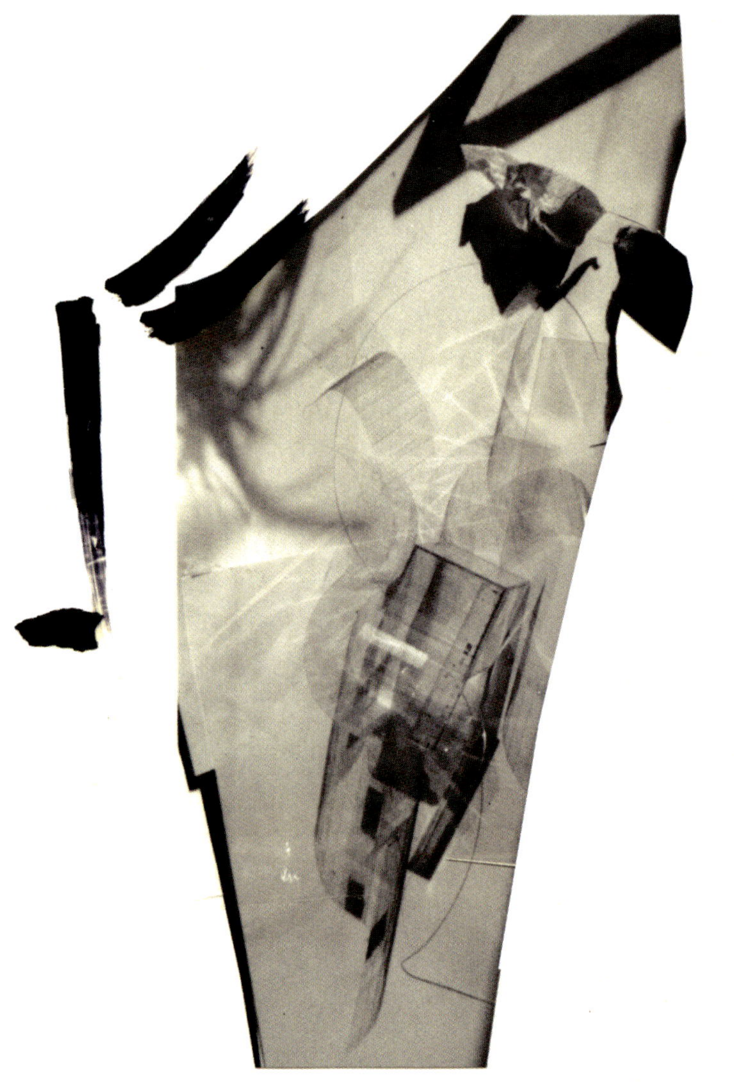

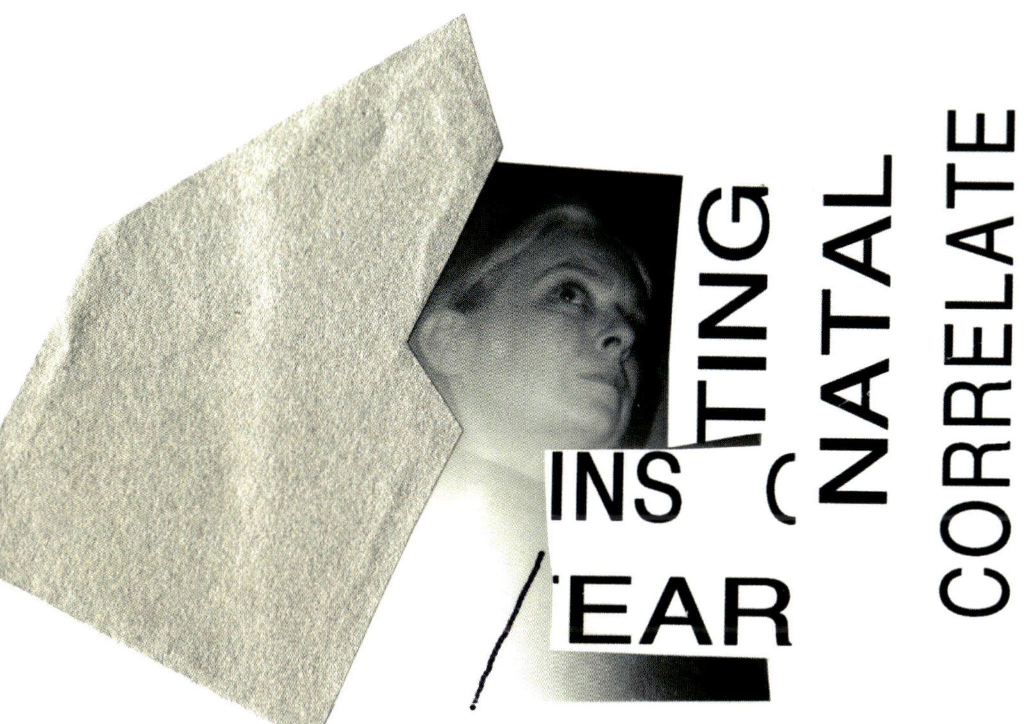
TING
NATAL
CORRELATE
INS
C
TEAR

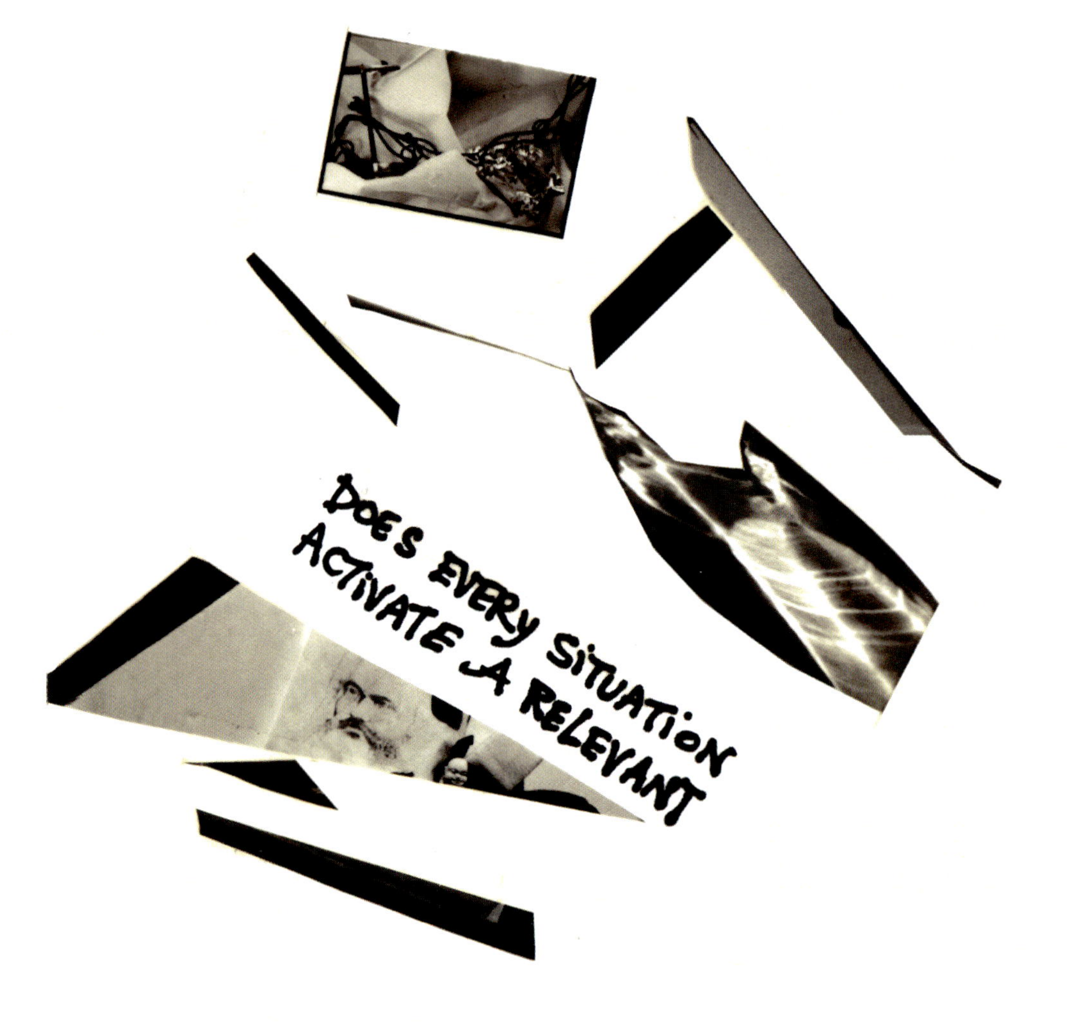
DOES EVERY SITUATION
ACTIVATE A RELEVANT

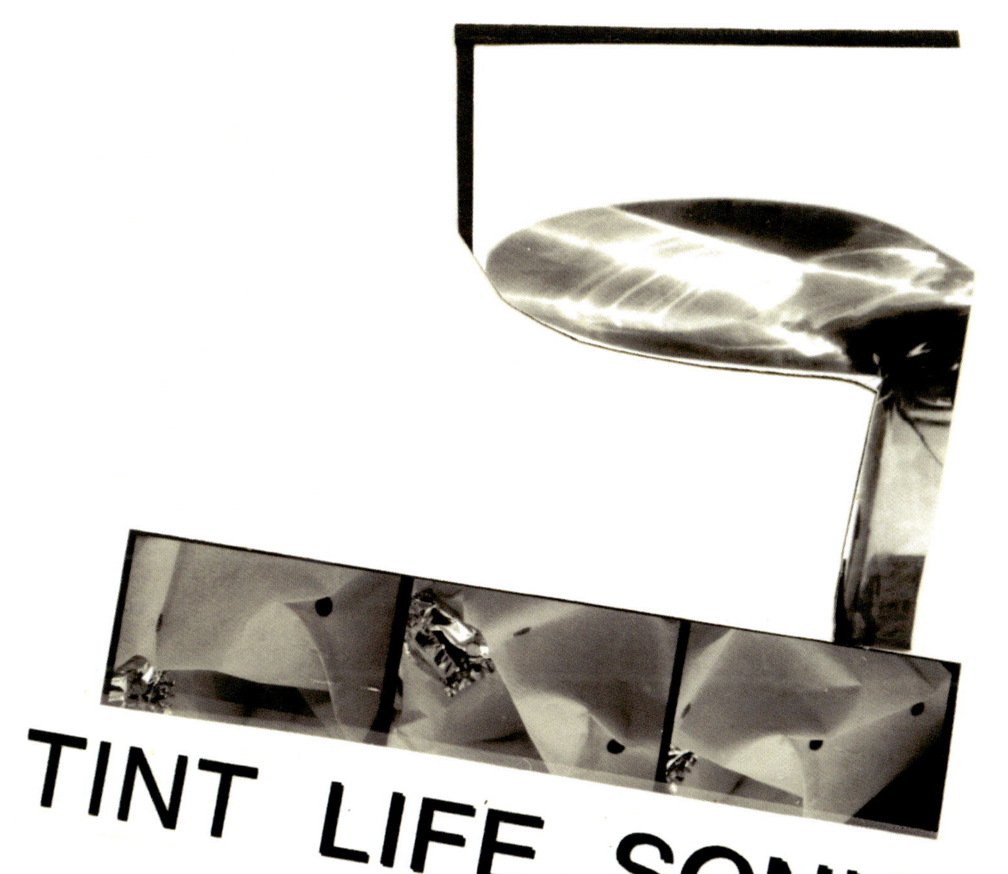
TINT LIFE SONIC

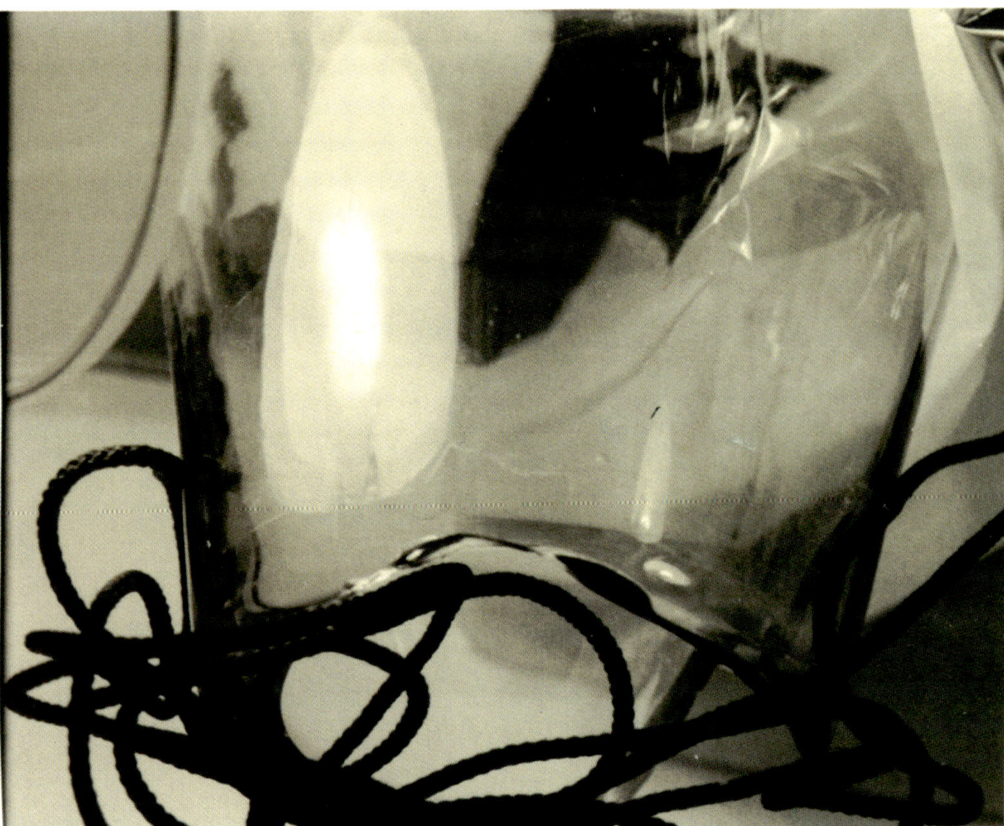

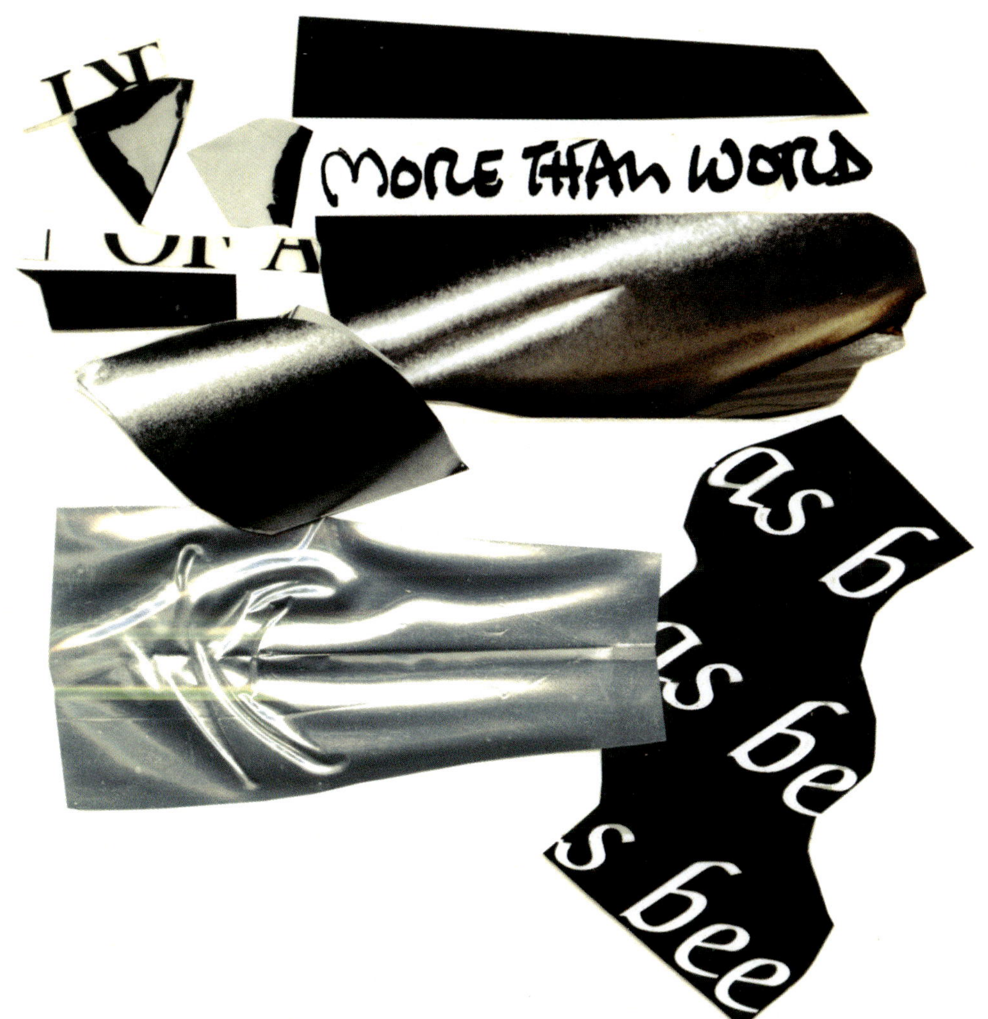
MORE THAN WORD
as b
as be
s bee

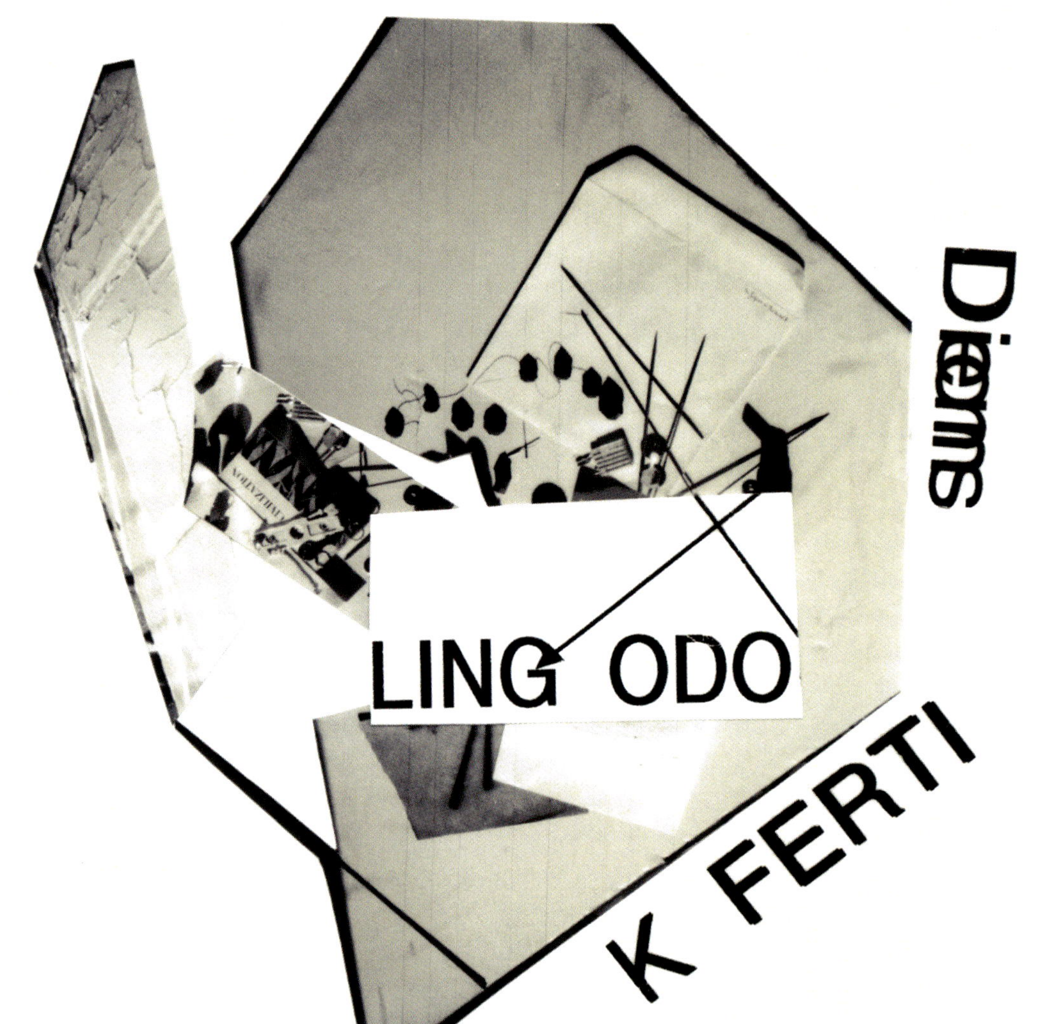

Diœms
LING ODO
K FERTI

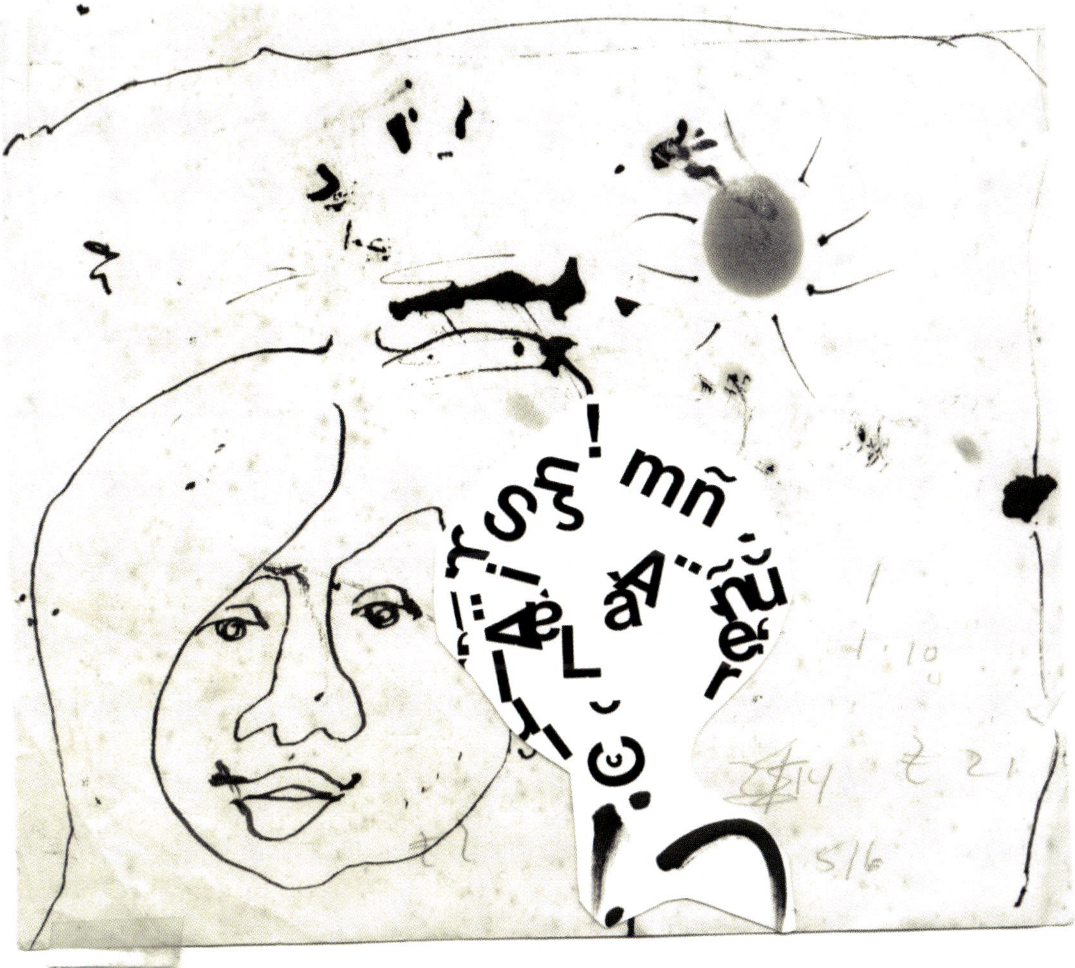

cogito the mirror stage, illuminative mimicry of the Aha
Kohler situational apperception rebounding in a complex
libidinal dynamis
ontologically virtual ontological structure
paranoiac knowledge imago specular specular "infans"
exhibiting in an extemporary situation
     symbolic matrix, precipitated in primordial form
objectification in the dialectic of identification
     making for jubilant assumptions
sunk in motor incapacity nursling dependance
     its predestination to a phase effect
     transformati
takingplace in the subject when he or she assumes image
And I'm only on page one of Jaque Lacan's linguistic

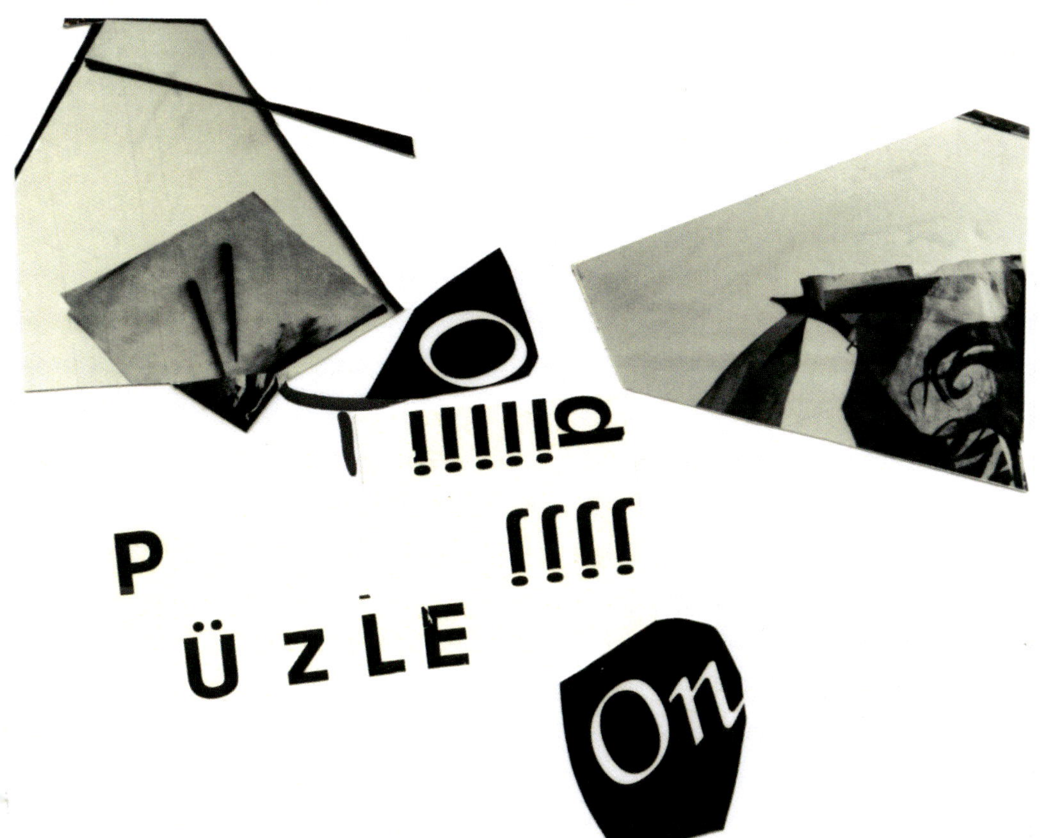
P
Ü Z L E
On

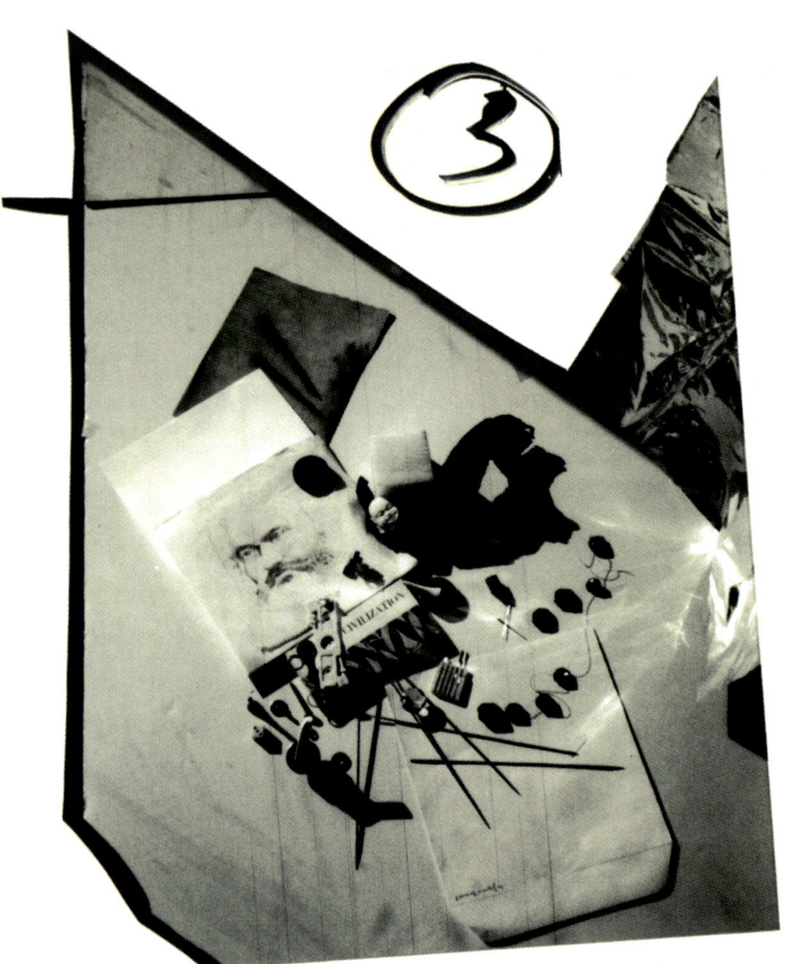

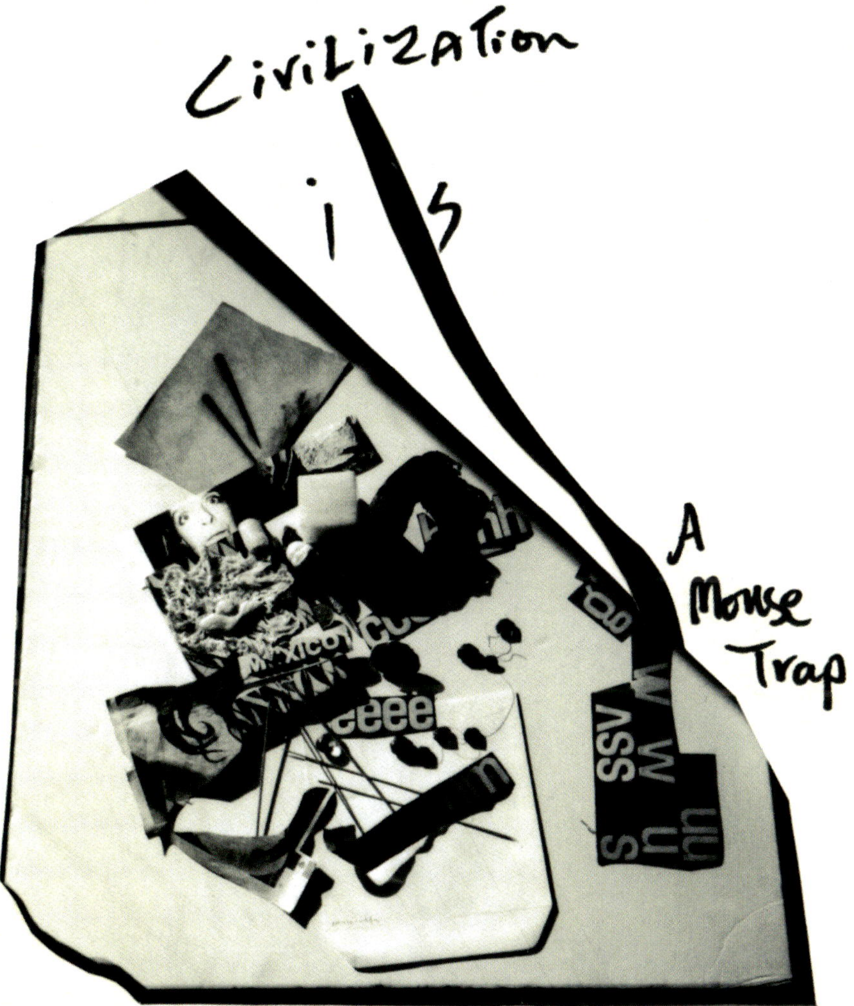

CiviLizaTion
is
A Mouse Trap

DOOR SLICK

SELDOM DOOM

FEBRILE TIGHT

SMOKE SINGED

E N T R

A P P D E

s!

If, due to secular fatalism, history is codified as
successful in itself, this may be due to a lack of
recognition of time-space continuum in which human being
situated. This I relate to Yogic science. The development
of the human being, by now possibly entirely genocidal,
occurs in conjunction with a basic misapprehension. The
poet occasionally touches upon the actual time base and
space but falling for the lie of the relentless push of
history becomes trapped. Efforts to cope with human
history end as didactic, evasive, enfeebled by compromise
with arbitrary aesthetic, subservient to a truely tiresome
individuality, plus escapist use of theoreticals. All
these efforts confine poetry and demean its ritual
signifying power.

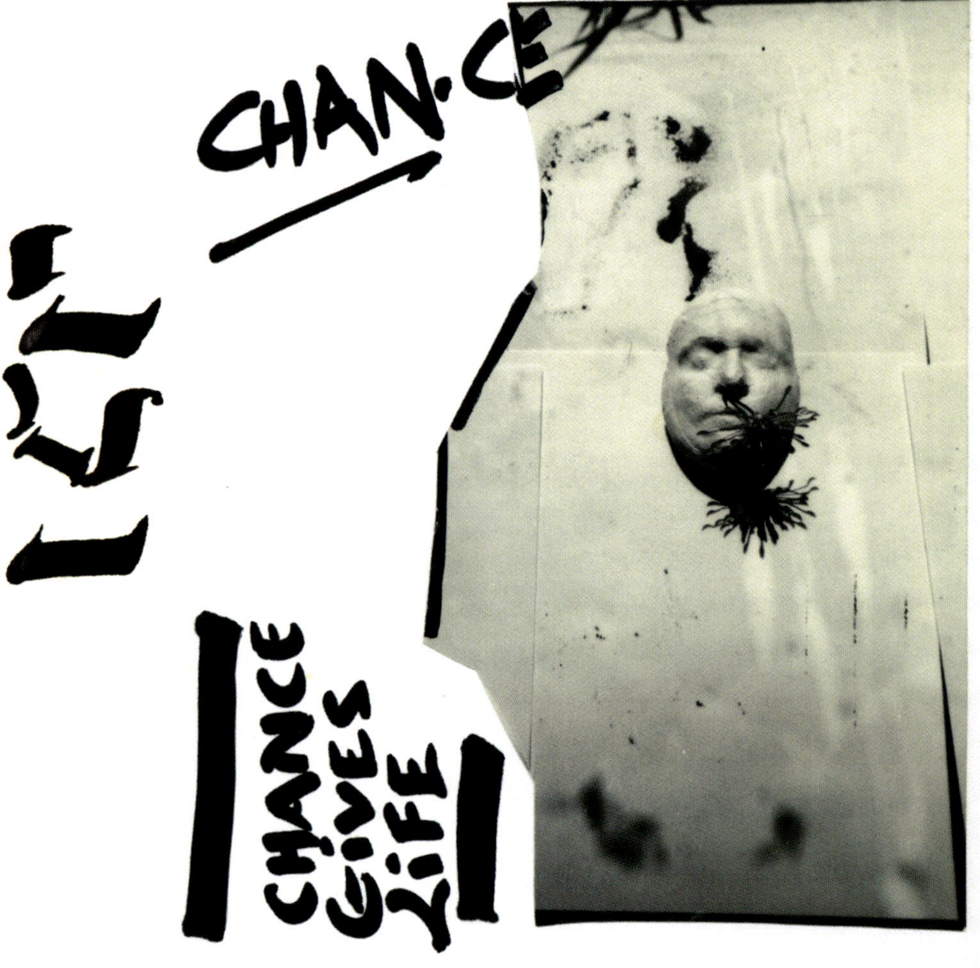

CHAN·CE
CHANCE GIVES LIFE

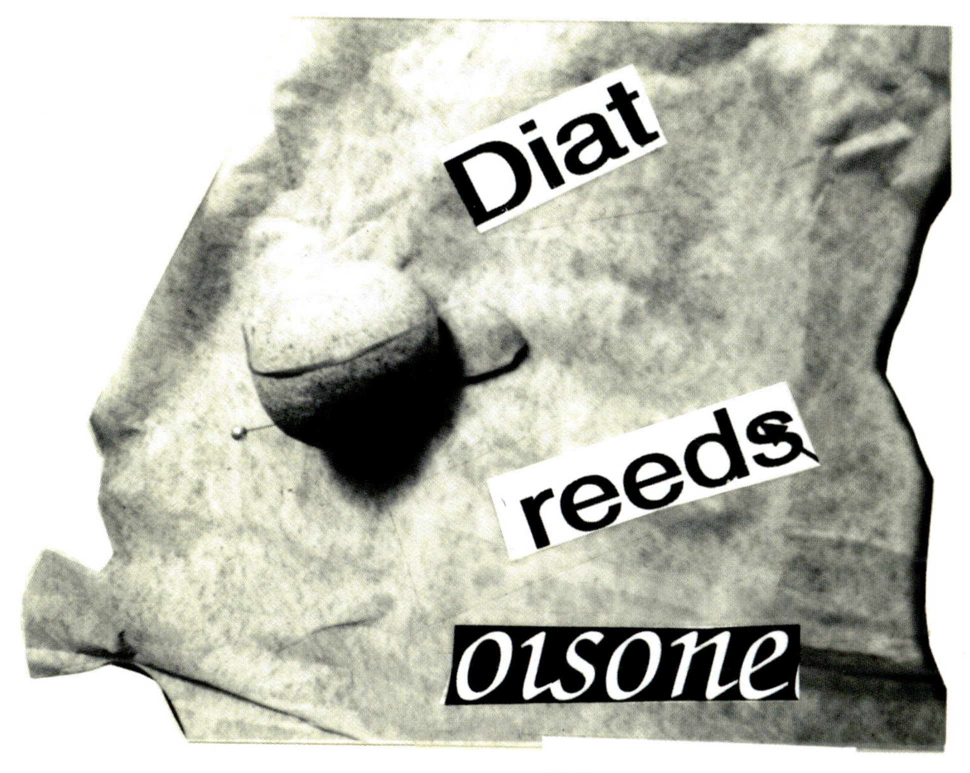
Diat
reeds
oisone
liett Rii

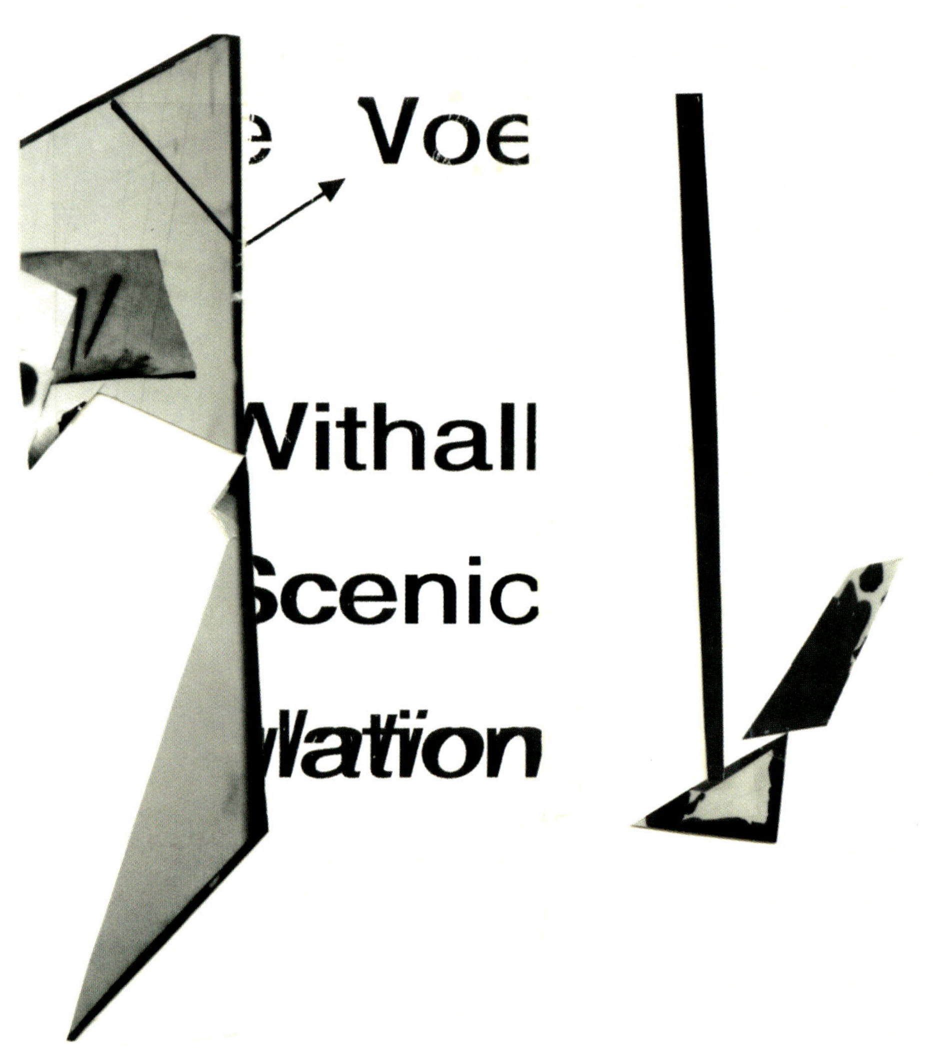

Voe
Withall
Scenic
Vation

SLOPE CRUDE

SLOOP *LISSOM*

CERTIFICAT SOUL

MUSIC SHELLING

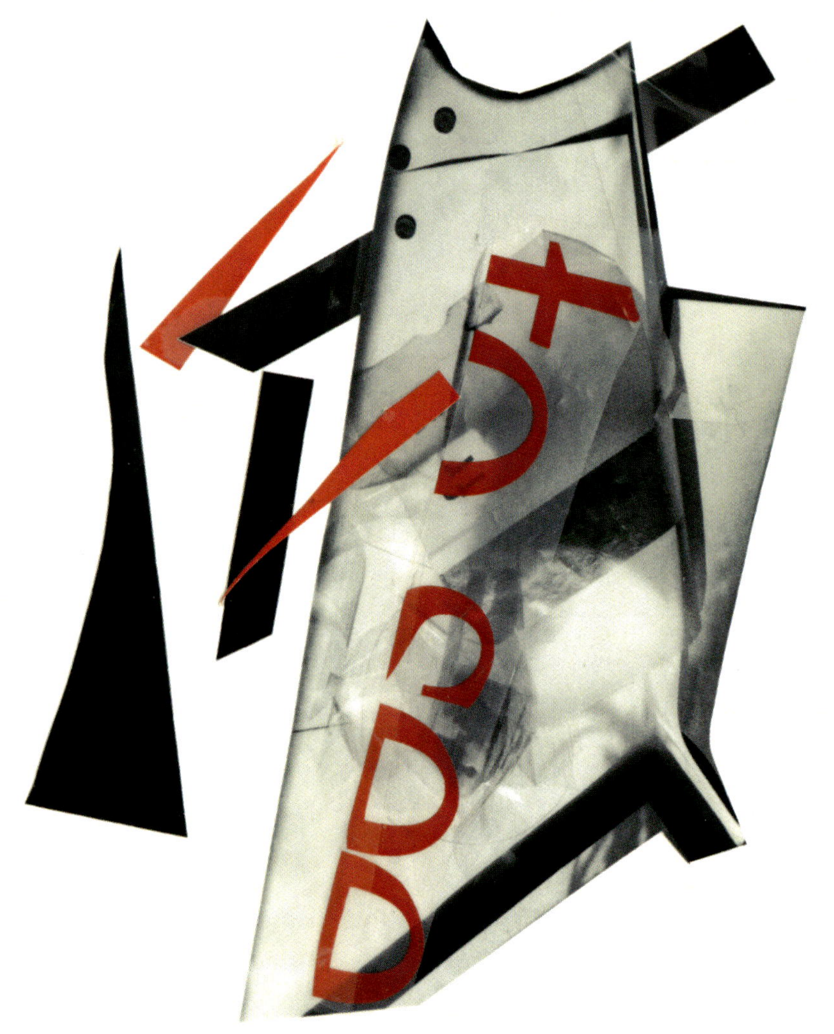

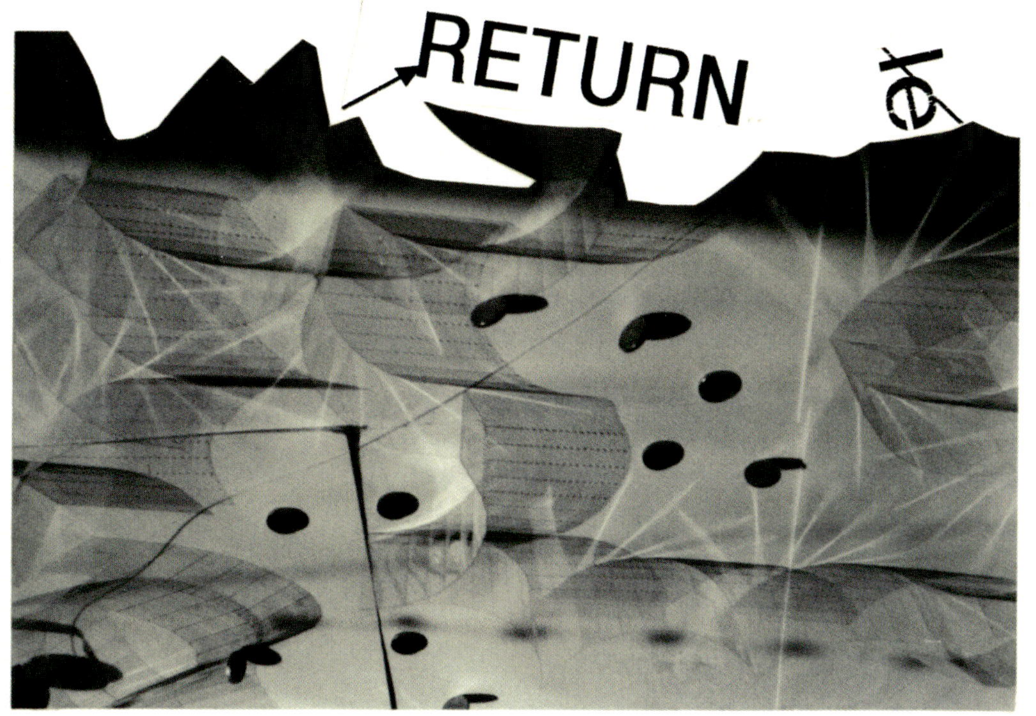
RETURN

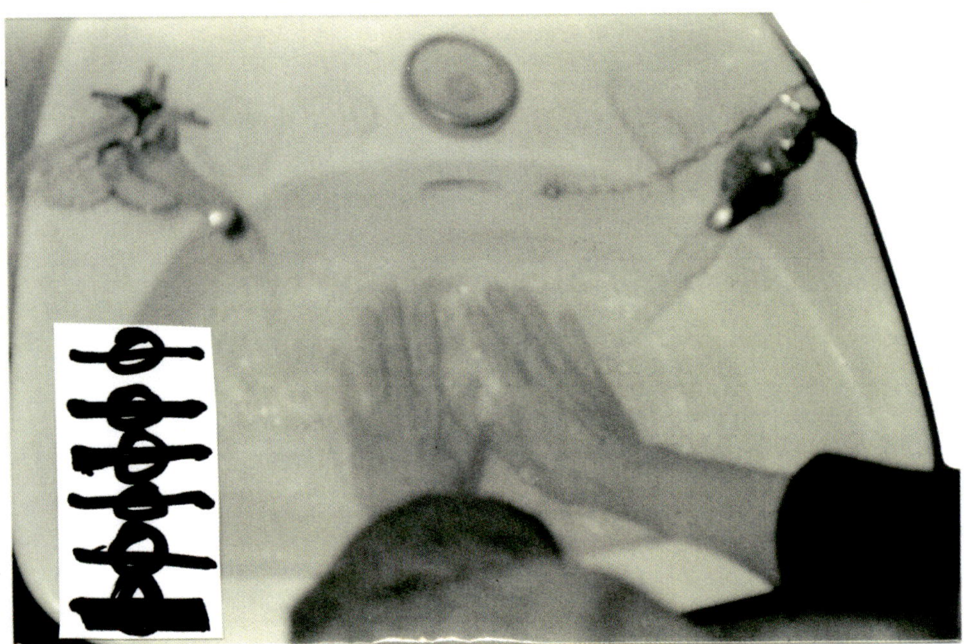

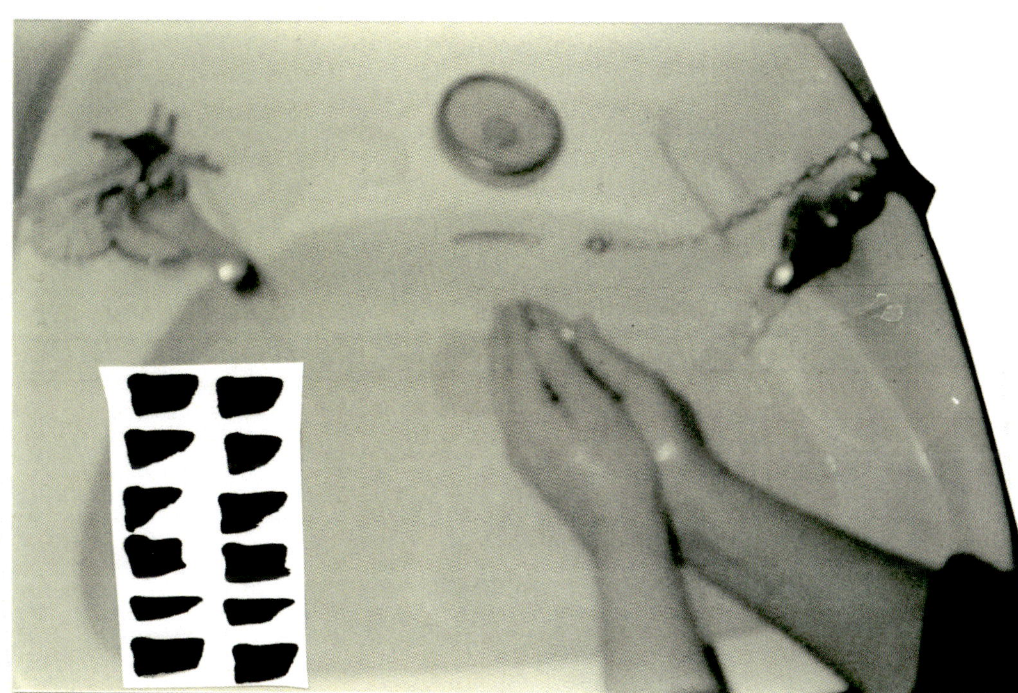

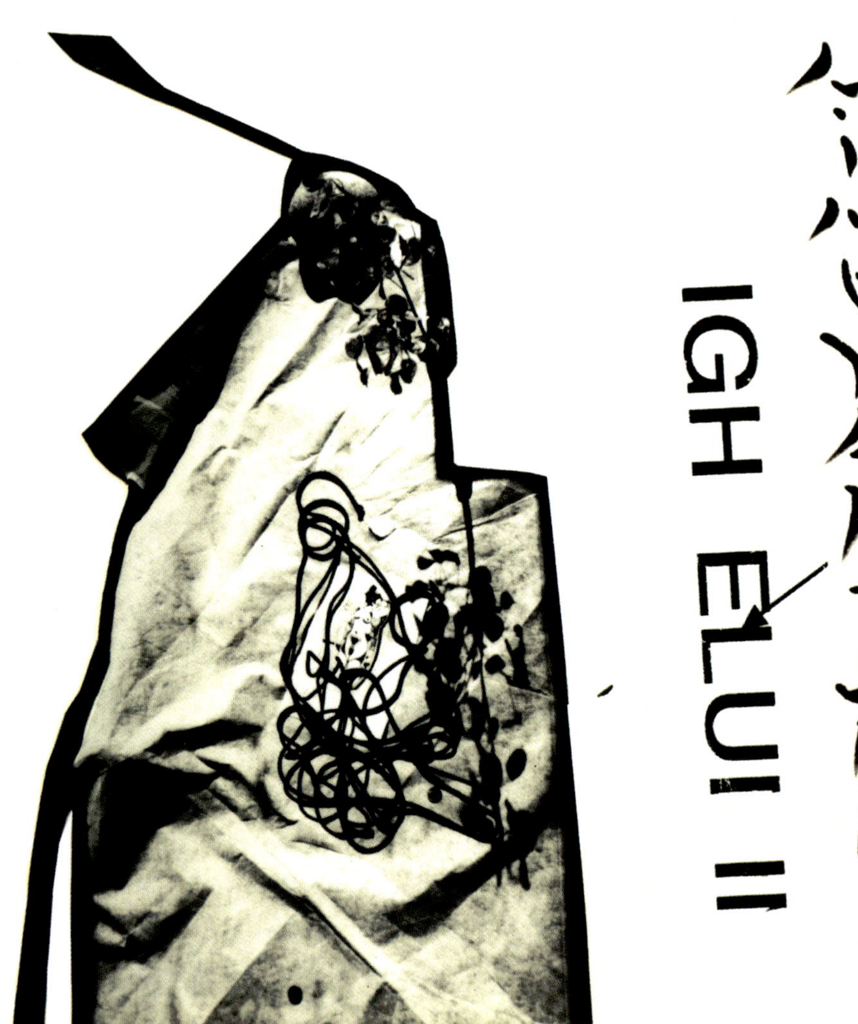

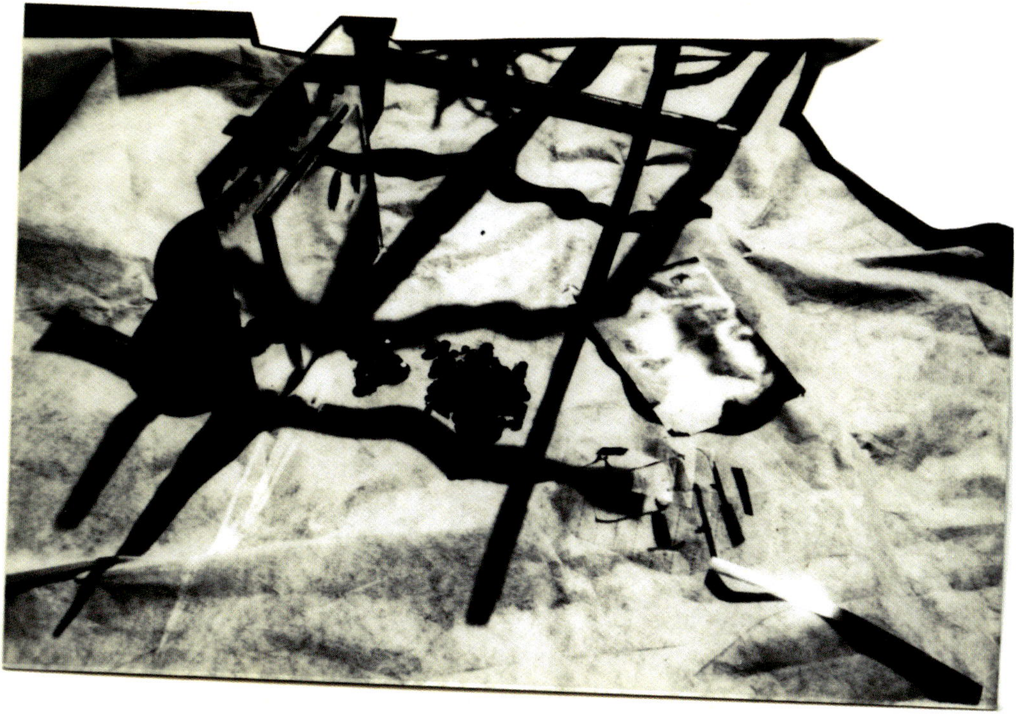

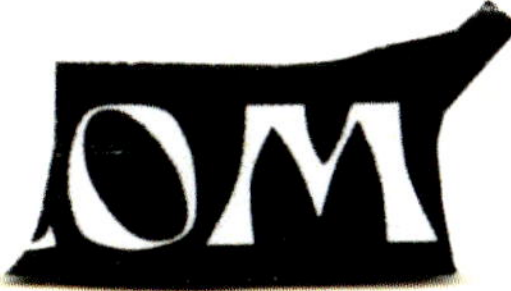

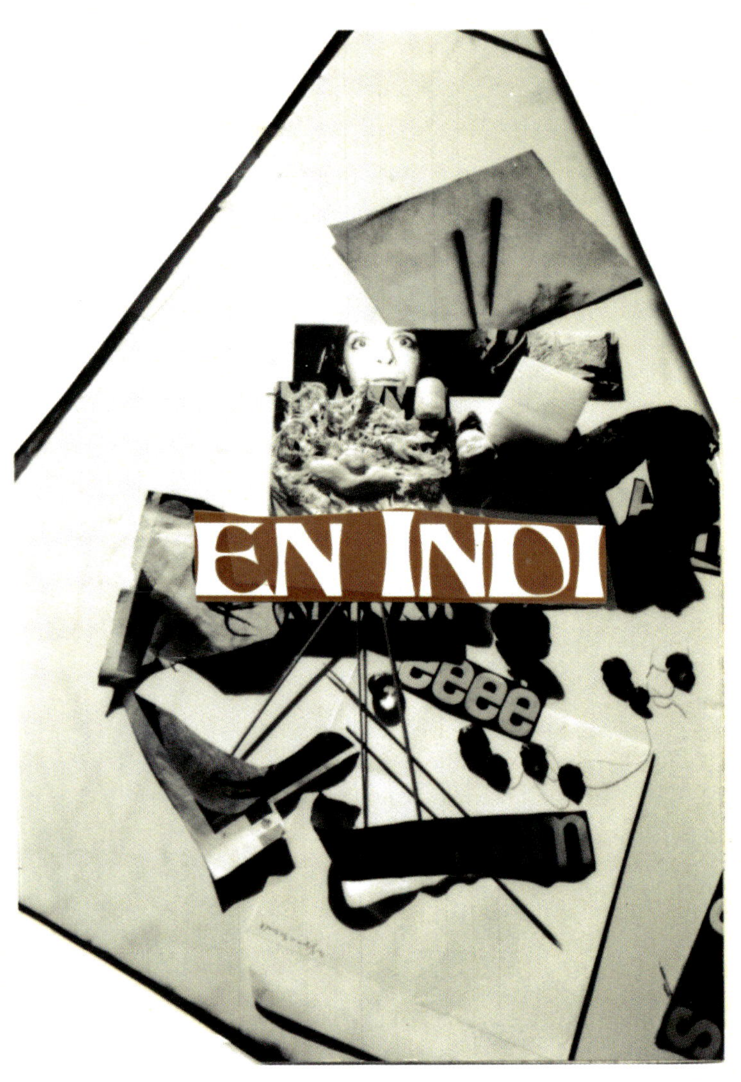
EN INDI

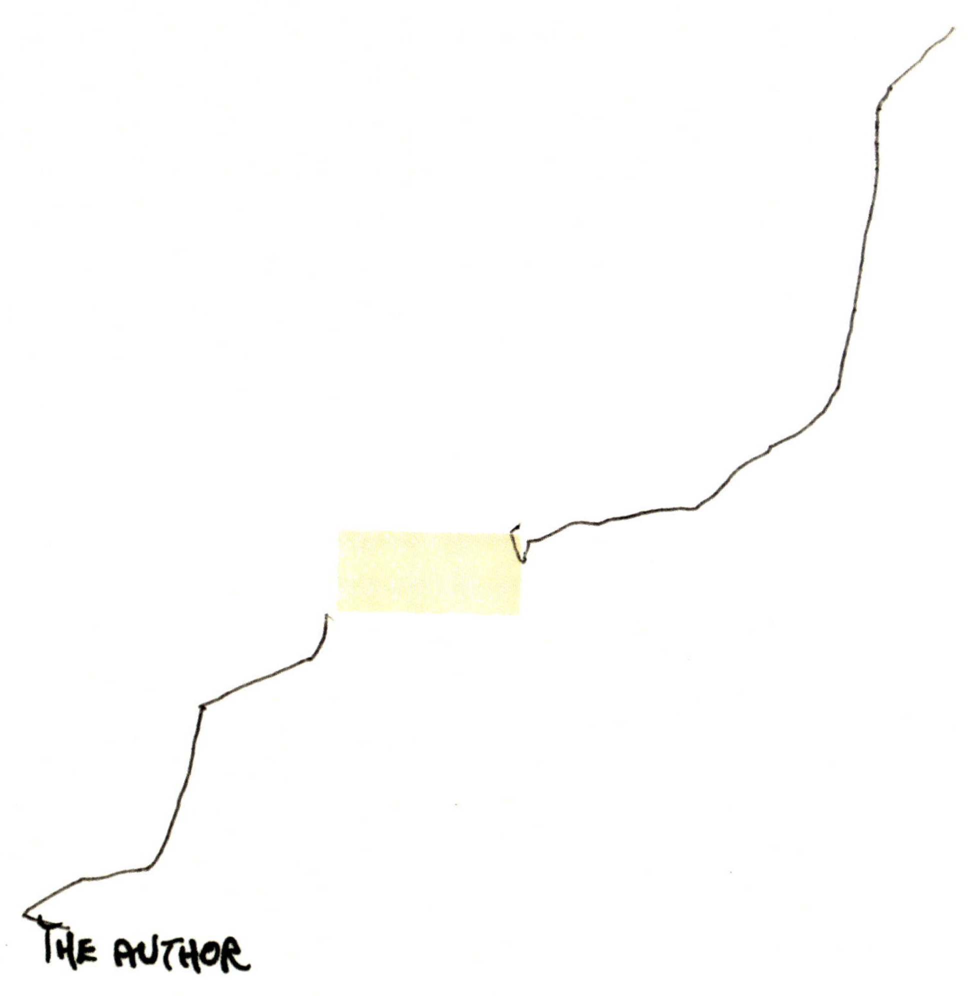

THE AUTHOR

SETTING A VALUE ON EVERYDAY HAPPENINGS
THE PROBLEM RECORDED THEN FOLDED
AN IMAGE IN AMPLIFICATION/REDUCTION
MULTIPLICATION free MINUTAE.
OVER BYES AND BYWAYS
UNDER THE RISE SIGHS
BOUNCES ALONG WHITE wrought iron
HEDGEROWS STACK UP CUBOID PROPORTIONS
MISSED THE SPEAKER THE SPEAKER SIGHS.
HIS CRIES COME POSTED ON THE AIR WAVES.
LIGHT
POSTED

E WHITE FUR KITFIDLERS
E FLYING. YOUR BEST C
ET Y IS A MYSTERY YOUG
TTHIN. LOOK DOWN LOOK
OU RUN WILD ALONG TH
IST BY THE SEA. IT IS

PERSPEX (any) NEW IDEAS
FLAT TIME FLATTENED,
EANING YOU CAN TRAVEL AT
AS THO YOU ARE PRESSED
EN 2 INCH-THICK 8" TALL
DEX. YO... "GET FLAT"
... e IS ROOM
... . YOU
... & indulge ... Inteli-
formation of ... space-
necessary. ... nate now
... lity precedence over

Space-Time T[...]

Trajectories in[to] space
at any angle, with NUMEROUS
Trajectories You are begin

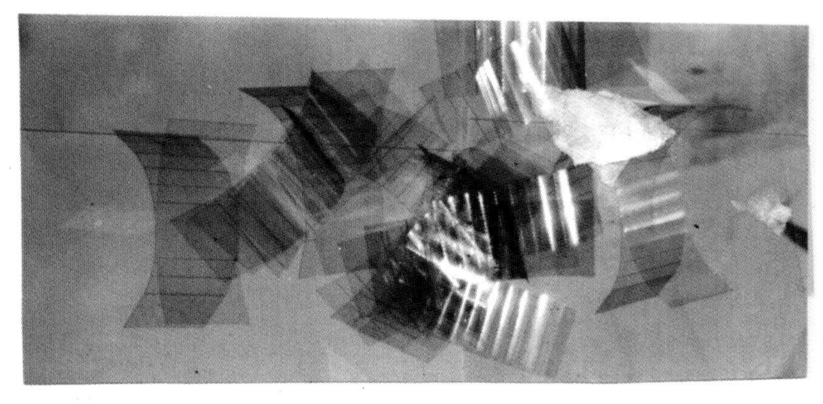

Amplitude of depth, from side to side, a perhaps infinite numbering to visualize it.

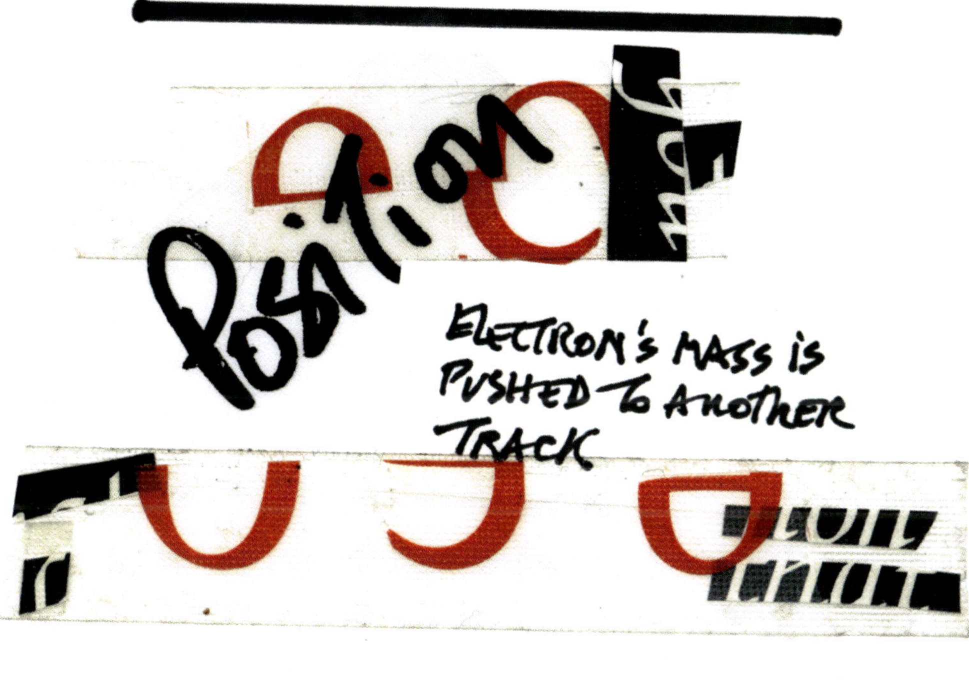
Position
ELECTRON'S MASS IS
PUSHED TO ANOTHER
TRACK

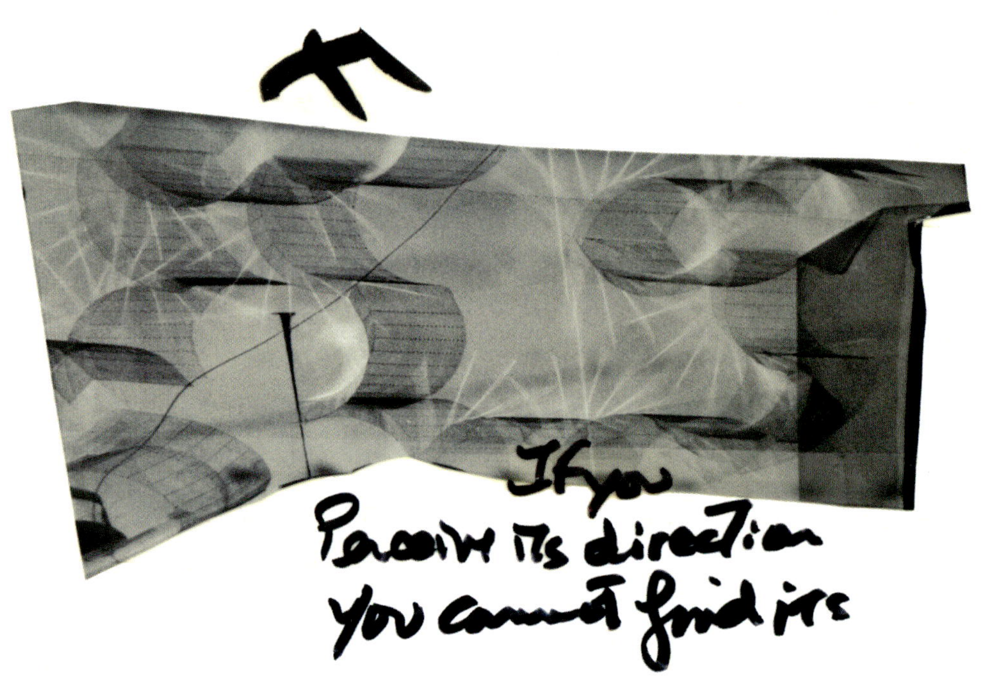
If you
Perceive its direction
you cannot find its

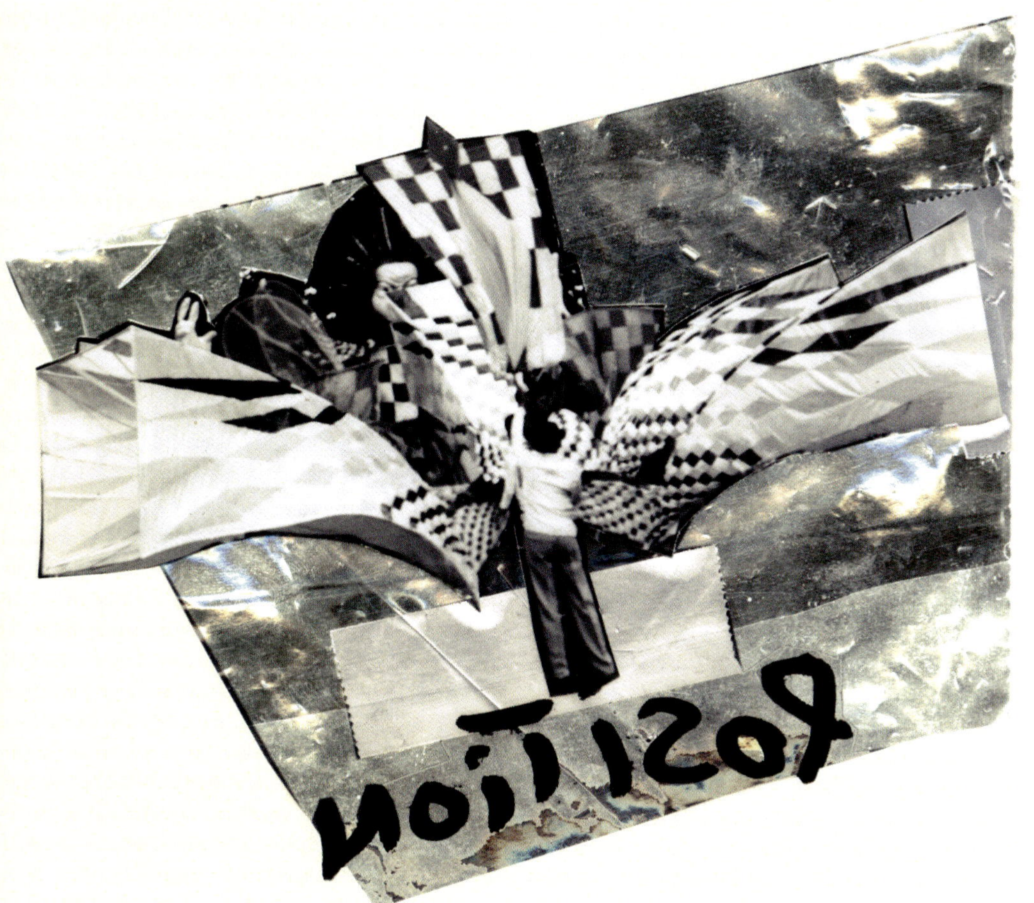
Position

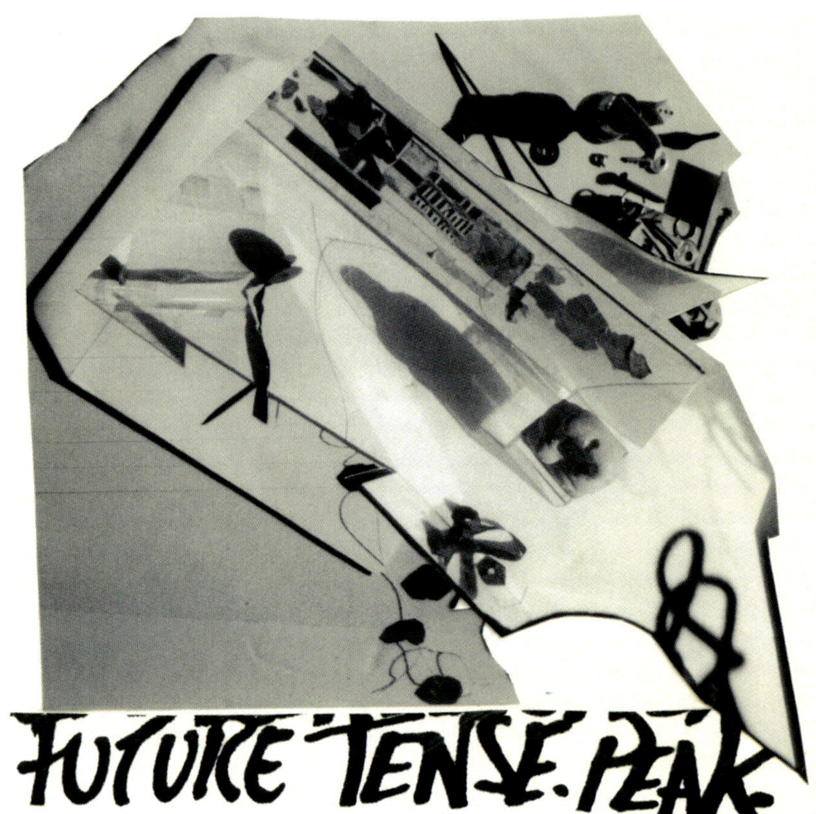
FUTURE TENSE. PEAK

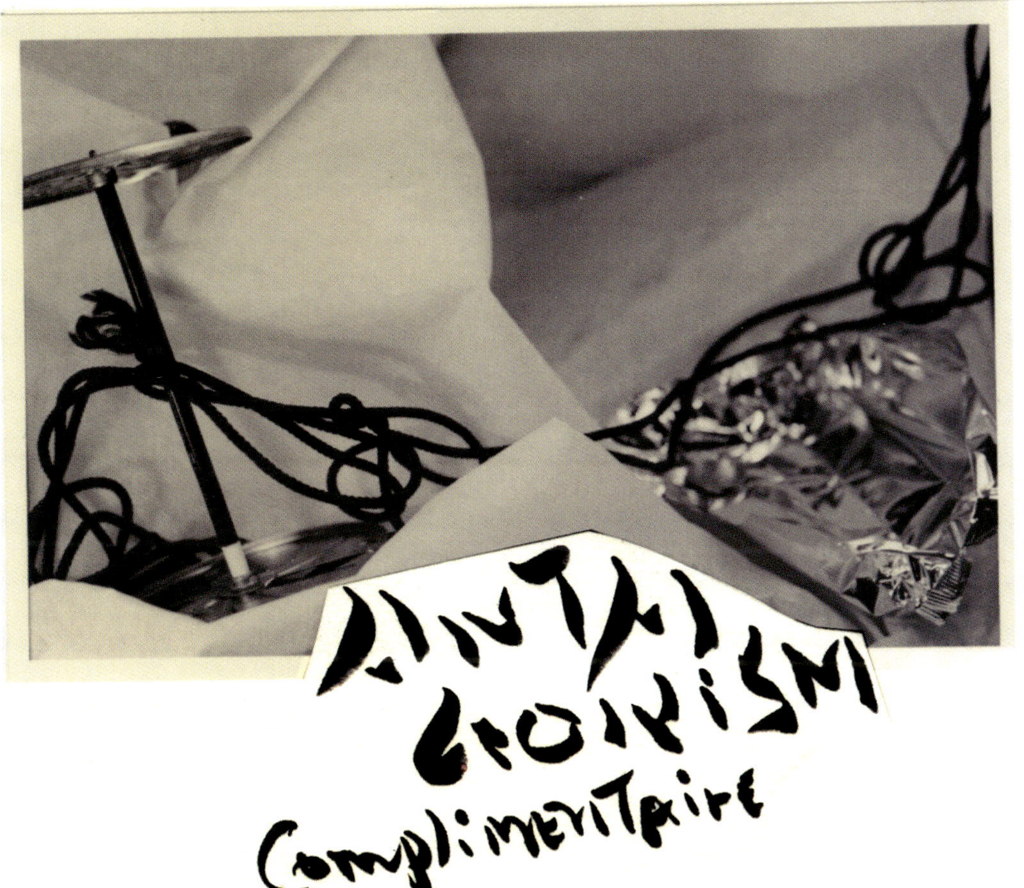

ANTAGONISM
complimentaire

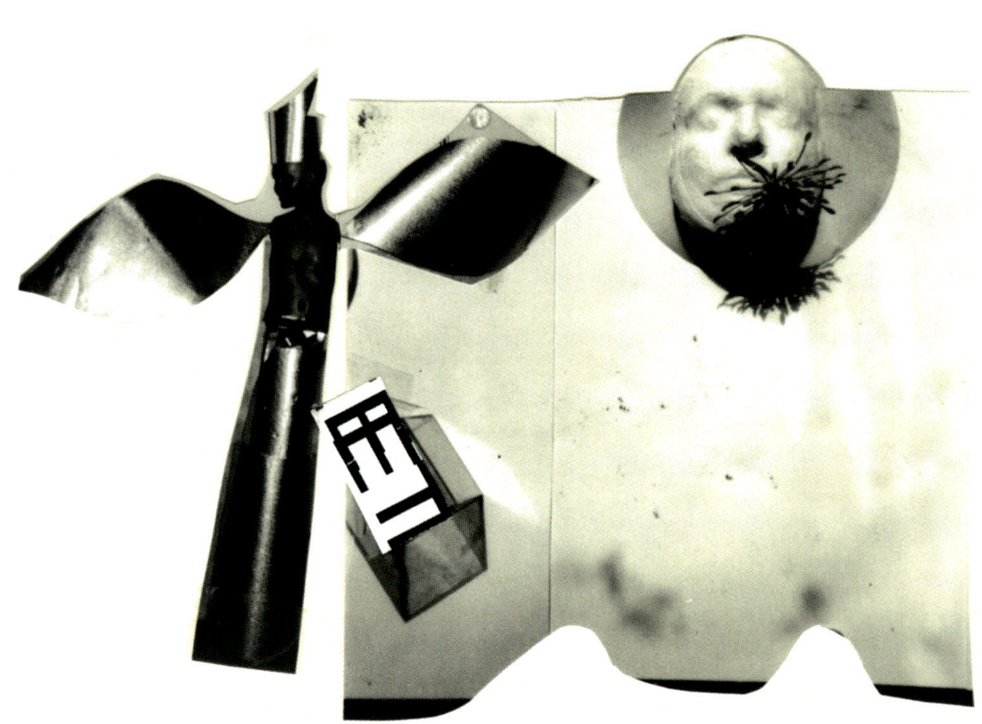

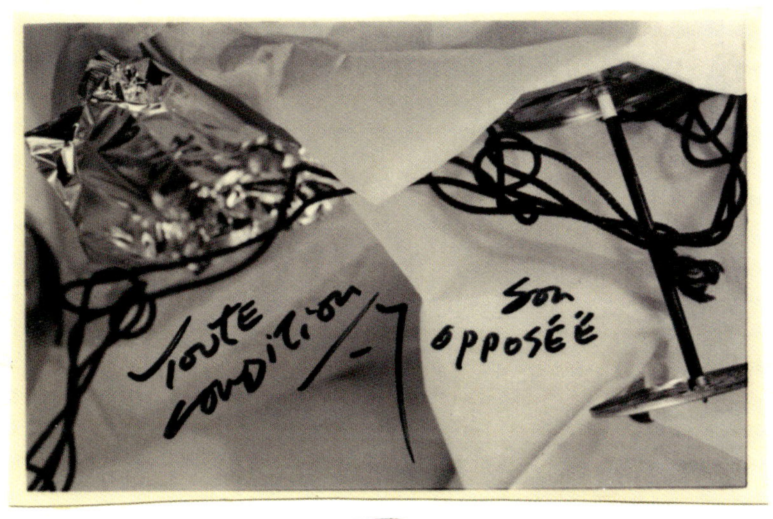

TOUTE
CONDITION A
SON OPPOSÉE

AFTERWORD

Alaric Sumner was my close friend, colleague and fellow-poet, generous-spirited, contemplative, sociologically re-appraising, intelligent, witty and patient. He was an active force in the Gay Liberation Movement as early as 1972. His productions for the stage were brilliant, as had always been his dynamic, self-discovering texts.

Alaric entered my life around 1977 when he was publishing his innovative *words worth* magazine. We re-animated a soul to soul dialogue after about a decade of separation. By then he had become very active with his own exciting creations, yet he took much time and put great effort into making certain that more people would come to know my work in art, theatre and poetry. He conducted discerning interviews with me, filmed my hands at work and published articles on my work.

EPOS, a Song For Alaric is a result of his death on March 24th 2000. Because he died very suddenly my side of our dialogue continued. I needed a language for speaking into absence. The creation of the "Song" is made with mobile components representing incidents, ideas and topics within a luminosity and shadings. I hope I have done justice to my friend, and resonated my sense of humour with his, wherever he is among the atoms on Porthmeor Beach.

Carlyle Reedy, September 2012

exhibition at <u>etruscan books</u>

<u>etruscan books</u>   Tuff Talk Press
2nd Floor, Oak Passage Studio   in   28 Moor Grove
68 George Street   association   Lawrence Weston
Hastings   with   Bristol BS11 0LR
Sussex TN34 3EE
<etruscanpublishing@gmail.com>
<robertthebard@blueyonder.co.uk>
www.e-truscan.co.uk

ISBN 1-901 538 86 9; 978-1-901 538-86-1

Epos, A Song for Alaric

First published by <u>etruscan books</u> 2013

Cover design by Robert W. Palmer using materials created by the Author.

Typeset by Robert W. Palmer at Tuff Talk Press, Bristol

Printed and bound by Colin Sackett, Axminster.

Found within the images are a trace-drawing of Karl Marx by Peter Healey Smith. Cover photograph of the author by P. Fisher.

The publication of *Epos, A Song for Alaric* was in part made possible by a grant from the Arts Council, England.

LOTTERY FUNDED   ARTS COUNCIL ENGLAND   Supported using public funding by

<u>etruscan books</u> are distributed by S.P.D., 1341 7th Street, Berkeley CA, 94710, USA, and are available from Collected Works, Level One, Nicholas Building, 37 Swanston Street, Melbourne 3000, Australia. <collectedworks@mailcity.com>

Other books by Carlyle Reedy:

Sculpted in this world (Bluff Books) 1979

The Orange Notebooks (Reality Studios) 1984

"I Live in a Land Where the Sun is Feminine." – Dialogue:
Carlyle Reedy and Joanna Jones (Arnoldshe, Frankfurt) 1993

Obituaries and Celebrations (words worth books) 1995

The Kiss (Paper Moth) 1996

etruscan reader iv with Bob Cobbing and Maurice Scully,
(<u>etruscan books</u>) 1999

Epos, Selected Poems (<u>etruscan books</u>) 2012